MEAT SCIENCE
ESSAYS

Michael McClure

Second Edition
Enlarged

City Lights Books

★

Other books by the author :
HYMNS TO ST. GERYON And Other Poems
                                    (Auerhahn Press)

DARK BROWN (Auerhahn Press)
THE NEW BOOK/A BOOK OF TORTURE (Grove Press)

GHOST TANTRAS

★

A number of these essays have appeared before : *Drug Notes* in EVERGREEN REVIEW, *Revolt* in JOURNAL FOR THE PROTECTION OF ALL BEINGS, *Phi Upsilon Kappa* in KULCHUR and FUCK YOU/A MAGAZINE OF THE ARTS, *Reason* in KULCHUR, and *Defense of Jayne Mansfield* in FILM CULTURE.

Third printing, October, 1970

CITY LIGHTS BOOKS are published at the City Lights Bookstore, 261 Columbus Avenue, San Francisco 11, California, U.S.A.

A Note on
MEAT SCIENCE ESSAYS

★

This spate of sense-thought, these romantic, intuitive non-essays will rub an awful lot of people the wrong way, as they have the editor of this book who doesn't at all agree with McClure's lush green ideas.

This editor is the friend referred to herein (in 'The Man in the Telephone Booth : *A Footnote on Camus*') and it's obvious to him that McClure doesn't want to understand Camus and never will. The cat is just willfully incapable of it. His whole book is, in fact, an evasion of that very 'suicide and death' which Camus' *Myth of Sisyphus* aims so Absurdly to confront. McClure's wildly opposite view is nevertheless one which many anti-intellectual (non-Gallic) animals will dig. McClure's 'mammalism' is something you just have to take or leave, along with his tacit presumption (in 'Artaud : Peace Chief') that the perceptions of madness (as in Artaud's 'To Have Done With the Judgment of God') are naturally greater, truer, more profound, etc, etc, than those of any other state of meat, mind, or heart . . .

Afterthought, three years later : What I said above still remains true for me; but it is still an important book.

— Lawrence Ferlinghetti

★

PREFACE to the Second Edition :

Thanks to Lawrence Ferlinghetti for inclusion of the three additional essays in this edition, making this the complete *Meat Science Essays*. The censorship problem kept the *fuck* essay out of the first edition — thus proving that censorship prevents criticism of itself. I began these essays by writing *Phi*

Upsilon Kappa. The others might be read as continuations of this newly-included essay. Essays are a stasis of a given stream of thought at any given moment. I have not changed the essays in any way. I hope they press towards a blue velvet eternity. . . .

— Michael McClure

CONTENTS

Meat Science Essays are dedicated to Keera & America

PHI UPSILON KAPPA

I've been through personal agonies that all men must go through. Writing this is a kind of pain as well as a joy at the chance to make a new liberty. Gregory Corso asked me to join him in a project to free the word FUCK from its chains and strictures. I leap to make some new freedom. I believe in a visionary philosophy that demands I take this chance and make a personal speech and statement. I know no languages but words of French, German, Latin and Greek that come from smatterings of school and reading. In my own investigations the Anglo Saxon language, Old English, is the most perfect tower and cavern of words I've yet discovered. I have emerged from a dark night of the soul. I entered into it by peyote and a propensity within myself that was brought to extreme by the cactus drugs. I emerged but still felt a fear that arose when I saw light radiating from the inorganic universe — the light that gleams from a plaster wall, or a brick, or chair, or old stool of dark wood. Constantly I saw all lights that flare and glisten stilly from objects. There were visions of man freed of time and born again as the beast and titan that he is within each Olympian set of genes-unique. Delusions and fear accompanied the sight.

Sometimes I would find myself snapped into a state of partial hallucination and tormented sight. Part of my suffering was that recognizing the timelessness of the Universe and man, I damned fear of mortality as contemptible sickness. I felt all cowardly acts to be fear of death. Life is not sacred only boldness is — *I thought*. The death we know is the gestures that are undone by fear. All actions are perfect and immortal. They can only be judged by intent and boldness. I envisioned

Eternity as an infinite statuary of acts. My inability to perform any act of desire or want, and my fear to live out the concepts that I dreamed of, added to my anguish. The light-from-objects reminding me of worse times caused exhaustion and more fear. The memory itself was a new and damning fright. Childlike blankness would settle on my mind and strike out both fear and human feelings. The image of my body wavered and became inexact. I swelled to soul hugeness and delusions of physical grandeur and vacuity. With my dark night vision had come the knowledge that we have no minds and are only spiritmeat. Meat, spirit, and *gene* are one and there is no time or size! I hallucinated that there is no *time* because it is a tool invented by corruption and domestication, of gene and spirit. I knew there is no mind because body is all. I no longer believe these things as I say them here. I am amazed at the pain and yearning of the search for total spirit and new universes of spirit. . . . I sweated into a tiny and infinite void.

As it all ended I saw my soul and found that I lived once before and that I had been a killer whale. I have had but one life before. At the end of this one I shall be free of the chain of meat. When I saw this I wept for long-lived men and for my daughter. (My freedom I know is a coincident of Time & Space.) I saw that there is no evolution in a single life. Death is good and black and painless and beautiful. I shook with the urge to die, staring through my black October window. I would have died but I realized that if all is good, and painless, and ecstatic sweet, and black on the other side of death, then this side of death is good also. There is no evolution in the personal sense. There is no graduation through suffering. The soft, soft, beauties of Anacreon and Jesus are as true as blacker ecstasies and are of the same matter and fleshmeat. I say these things as I have just turned 28 and I speak them while still suffering sometimes from a blankness that causes me anguish. But I have found idealism and sight of beauty that I cherish in deepest new depths.

I felt inspiration coming. I was shaken by it and realized I had no words to speak what was growing in me. I mulled in the books of Melville (his holy novel *Pierre*) and read the works of great poets of our language and other men I knew. Still I could not find more than beginnings of the words I needed. I looked in the plays of Shakespeare and found his sweet wise imagewords, and the behemoth metaphors he makes with use or turn of word — how he gives everything noble stature by his suddenness and humor. I could not find in words anywhere the counterpart of what I felt within myself that lay unspoken and building in intensity. By instinct while searching through books of words, because of a memory of great sounds I heard in poetry of that language, I turned to Anglo Saxon and I began leafing in dictionaries of that speech.

Almost first I opened to the word *aelf-scin* — *shining like an elf*. The reference was to the light that gleams from objects! This is the light I saw at many moments and for extended lengths of time. It threw me into fear and blankness. It was the real visionary horror of the inert world about to become hallucinatory vision. BUT if those great Anglo Saxon men saw the light and named it — natural phenomena — *then what is there to fear from it? What is there to fear from elf-light? From elf-scimmer?*

THE AELF-SCIN, THE SHINING SCIMMER, THE GLEAM, THE SHINING
color of walls, of scratches, of cracks, of brightness.
The cold mystery the (Philip calls it) Weir. The *déjà vu* of the forest-sorrel with its tiny leaves sun-folded
and bent like a head in uniqueness. Animal in look
to fold so. The moment I
leave what I am in aelf-scin. Stand
in wonder. Lose myself. Even to fear.

A difference. Aelf-scin, Weir. But
similar. Knowing its name the horror
of void is gone. Knowing it almost
with my ash spear over my arm in the black
FOREST CLEAR WATER AND AIR SEA.
The Anglo Saxons build huge boats, fight battles
and rejoice in what they see,
see beauty more clearly,
have words for what
I forget, Live in
liberty. For
ever. ! ! ! ! !

CALL IT FEAR NOW-GONE
the whole thing a star
breathing.

Philip Lamantia and I had spoken many times. He had
mentioned his concept of Weir to me. Now I knew the phenomena I had seen with my still peyoted eyes — the chill luminescence — and the aelf-scin of the Anglo Saxons were the
same radiance and halo. I saw that the aelf-scin was much
the same light illumining what Philip called Weir. Weir is a
solid spectral reality of light on particular objects in special
moments of vision.

CALL IT FEAR NOW-GONE, the whole thing a star
breathing. The scar was gone and healed!

In dictionaries of Anglo Saxon and Old English, and in
dictionaries of forgotten languages of argot I found living and
vital images and titles for forgotten sights. A man names what
he sees and then puts away the fear of it.

In Old English I found a treasury of beauties that we still
may see but are without words for. The names are lost and
forgotten! The words make them more visible. I found black

grottos and cliffs of unremembered meanings and beings. In my state I swallowed them whole and saw new beings and wonders with cleansed eyes. I saw the fields of tiny radiances and color on the bloodied body of a mackerel that I roasted whole and ate. I saw the dead body of the living that I consume — loving animals and beasts. I saw myself eating them. I felt ˉmy stride and chest as I walked. I sat silently in the *daegred-woma* and the *morgen-rot* and listened to a child sing wild wordless songs of her desires. I thrilled with the ecstasy of my spirit's physicality. I knew all of the subtle and gross variations of day and dark. The fear of aelf-scin flew from me in a clap of joy when I discovered that the Anglo Saxons, rich in forest and sea, had seen it.

Their words opened new forgotten beauties to me :

aedel-tungol . . . noble star.

an-sund . . . whole sound (meatspirit solid, vibrant, solid moving, free).

ae-men . . . depopulated (not de-populated but *ae-men* — manless).

ad-loma . . . fire lamed.

adl-bracu . . . force or virulence of disease (*adl* is disease).

ae-craftig . . . law crafty.

aedre . . . artery, vein (it is the sound of a vein).

aefen-glom . . . evening loom, twilight, gloaming.

aefen-leocht . . . evening light.

aefen scimmer . . . evening shimmer, evening splendor.

aefen steorra . . . evening star.

aefen-tid . . . eventide.

ael-cald . . . all cold.

aeled . . . fire, firebrand, conflagration.

aeled-fyr . . . flame.

ael-grene . . . all green, green on all sides.

aeppel-fealu . . . apple fallow, apple yellow, red-yellow (Oh, joy to eat an apple !).

aerend-boc . . . message, letter.

aerend-gewrit . . . written message, letter epistle.

aer-mergen . . . daybreak.

aer-woruld . . . former world, old world, Ur Welt.

ae-sprynge . . . (1) waterspring, font; (2) what's to happen, fate, destiny.

aetran-mod . . . venom minded.

aedel cyning . . . noble king, Christ.

aedm . . . breathing (the sound of breathing?).

aewan . . . to despise, scorn, contemn.

an-floga . . . the alone, the lonely flyer.

agenslaga . . . ownslayer, self-slayer.

ar-craeftig . . . strong in honor.

ar-scamu . . . holy awe, respect.

bael-blaese . . . fire blaze.

bael egesa . . . flame feared, fire dread.

bael egesa . . . flame fear, fire dread.

ban-hus . . . bonehouse, body.

ban-sele . . . bonehall.

becn . . . signal, beacon.

bell . . . forehead.

bellan . . . bellow, bark, grunt.

beag-gifer . . . ring giving.

bealu, bealo, balu . . . bale, evil, mischief, hurt, injury, affliction.

bealu-blonded . . . mixed with destruction.

bealo-hycgende . . . thinking of death.

bealo-inwit . . . deceit, cunning, treachery.

bealo-sorg . . . sorrow because of expected misfortune.

bearthm . . . splendor brightness (what it is that impresses the senses, makes a sound, comes out strong and bright. What comes straight through the nerves and synapses of the body without the recirculation and channelings of habit and custom — straight from the spirit and unbuffered. A bodyspirit movement of any size or quality).

breost cearu . . . breast care, sorrow.

brun . . . having a metallic color, dark, black.

brunwarm . . . dark brown, dusky.

bryne . . . tear, burning tear.

calic . . . chalice, cup.

ceoldheort . . . cold hearted.

beo-bread . . . bee bread, honeycomb.

ceor . . . anxious, careful, full of anxiety.

cleo . . . claw or hoof.

clingan . . . cling, shrink draw up, pine, wither, become weak.

I did not find *fuck* in Anglo Saxon dictionaries — but it is no matter whether the word was used then or if it was born in later days of Old English. In books of forgotten words and images from other times I found more words to give me new pictures and sensations. Part of a man is the words leaping from his lips. They are made by his real meat lips and throat and signalled by his real physical hands of spirit sending them on their way. They are groomed by the features of his face — lips, crinkle of eye, and swelling and collapse of cheek and chin. They free and liberate and lead to deeds and constructions and inventions of soul and spirit. Active living men had seen what I was seeing. They knew aelf-scin and did not fear it — they named it. They freed me of fear. I wanted to live in the sights named in Anglo Saxon and old shapes of language. I felt what men who knew the earth, the wind, and boiling-cold sea, drew from the air and light and beasts around them. I reached to feel things named in their languages; intensities of life that are wealthy living. I felt my heart, my real actual heart of blood and muscles in the ribcase of my chest fed by and feeding its arteries and veins. I saw my capillaries rise in heat. I dreamed in gloaming and heard the cries that fill the eventide and saw the beastwoman creatures and animal men

that move around me (so many of them are not stirred to great
and noble deeds but they are still such vital spirits!). Speeches
and speech are part of living. Great plays of words can lead
to high actions. Pleasures of words make voluptuous ease and
needed rest and comfort and good sleeping for the mammal.
Heavens of voluminous colors and stalwart actions are caused
by sounds.

A man knows *what* he is by how he names his states. If I do
not name my condition I am less defined and lack sureness.
Speech cannot be censored without loss. Words are part of
physiology. Lost parts of body are losses of spirit. There are
men and women in honest suffering blaming themselves for
misery when the name or word of their torment will assuage
them. The mention of it is the first step to relief or cure —
but it is denied them by their social company who are joined
in a fear to use a word or hear it spoken.

One stanza of my poem *Dark Brown* begins:

OH EASE, OH BODY-STRAIN, OH LOVE, OH
EASE ME NOT! WOUND BORE
be real, show organs, show blood. OH let me
be as a flower. Let ugliness arise without care
and grow side by side with beauty. . . .

In the first line I named the pain remaining from my dark
night *Wound-Bore*. Previously I had no name for it. I christ-
ened it and gave myself that ease so I could know my state
and therefore be more whole. Why do we refrain from naming
our states?

Does lack of name and recognition of the spirit's true shape
make us vague and pale? I believe it.

No actions or doings of the spirit should be called ugly. Or
call some that, but remember they are living shapes and not
to be denied. Beauty and bliss are other states and often they
commingle. Ugliness, beauty and bliss if they are felt are to

be named. For the sake of what is humane there should be no repression of statement. Suffering as well as joy should be titled. Good and evil must be put to words. Each genetic immeasurable titan manbeast must name his names and the shapes visible to his senses. If he does not he is incomplete and less manly. Silence is a grey cloud of denial of life.

Denied hungers of the physical-gene-body are contradictions of spirit. Hungers for sex, food, loveliness, and love are manifestations of the spirit who is a manbeast. What is the concern with measurement and denial? A real physical spirit is not in scale. There cannot be a proportion claiming a star is a size and man is another size. They both are alive! There is no living relativity of scale! Measurement and denial are destroyers of immortality. Words are the body as they float from tongue to air to other meatspirit or listener.

The only secret of speech is the way it is used. The good of words is not known enough. There are no mysteries of speech, there is no mystic language. (There are holy languages and ones that are kept secret.) Words are tools of men. All words are true when used with freedom, goodwill and honesty.

There are men who deal in false mysteries. They are frightened and hope to shake away their fears by rigid denial. They pretend that certain words and acts do not exist (and thereby make them mysteries). Men who condemn a word cannot use it to feel the shape of their spirit. They are cloudy and weakened and grasp for power to reassure themselves. They battle constantly to remove a word's meaning from reality. As they deny reality of their acts and feelings, a blankness, a destruction of human feelings, comes over them. It is amputation. They are amputated men and they desire like the fox without tail to make all fellows tailless in their image. They believe they have secluded themselves from their fears but they have *lost* reality instead. They believe all men have fears equivalent to theirs . . . or that they *should* have. They wish to protect the abridgement of their spirit. They are unaware that they are not whole. They make a mystery of words — *fuck* and many other straight words. They are fearful of sex and fearful of cleansing. All men who deny are destroying their spirits. Who can measure the desires or speech of a man?

Everyone must speak and act with pride of reality so that each can construct in full his unique spirit. First we must be whole and *then* condemn evil if we see it. We must be free in graceful liberty to see and *then* make denial.

Cynicism, denial, and censorship create corporeal bulkheads and walls that dam the human spirit. We live in a vision, but only experience is true life. For a man to make his spirit whole he must smash up the terms of his own vision before the edges of it freeze and become unshifting. What we say and do creates the real actuality of our bodies. Our meat calls for that! If we are hung up in our existent visions or confined by another's, we freeze to a solitary and unchanging idea of ourselves. Then our universe of possibilities, our human universe, is dead. We must make love. We must constantly move and seek without denials or censorship or rigid fantasies. We are creatures enchained if we freeze up our vision to inflexibility. Locked words make closed men.

The obscenity barrier is raised by censorships and fear. It is built by a fear of the natural and the idea that nature is obscene.

The fear ridden man and the politician believe the normal and the common are obscene and would have men erect a wall in their spirit. They are the few possessors of unnatural fears and they live their lives of terror in hypocritic self-brutality. They desire stability and a quiescence of their scare. They want to reduce the possibilities of life to a living death to calm themselves. Natural and normal men and women terrify them. Fear gives energy and persuasiveness, and they persuade men to build a wall (the fear of obscenity) across their feelings. The

obscenity barrier freezes the spirit solid on the side that faces
the outer world and shuts up the nascent infinitude of acts and
loves on the other. ' Obscene ' is concerned with the cleaning
of the body or its processes of love and birth. Discoverers of
the obscene find death as unnatural as health and birth. They
erect mortuaries and hospitals as masonry to protect themselves from death.

Behind the wall of censorship lie possibilities that cannot
flow into the frozen and known and create new ideals. Mountain chains of loves and dim lovely valleys are walled away
without a gate. They are the desires for creativity and the
human divine. One stone of the barrier is the denial of true
and wholesome words. The unused walls become a solid force
within us and grow higher. The unchanging self is more cut
off and takes on terrible smugness as other worlds become
invisible. The smugness covers the pain of amputation. Any
man retreats from his uncountable creative possibilities if he
can be forced to fear acts of sexual beauty and to repress his
natural desires. What is there to fear? The free man only
desires to make himself whole. Fear of words is a symptom.
What seraph cities and cherubic bridges are still unbuilt because of denial and censorship that hold back energy? Is man
evil? Can spirit be evil? Is even ugliness to be as much feared
as beauty? Because of love of stability and unchanging vision,
what real dramas of love and kindness go unacted? How
strange to see the pettiness of spirit cloistered up with the aid
of unmade words. There are no mysteries of language or of
meat. Those who deny reality make mystic languages and
walls.

FUCK! The word fuck is a mantra. Sanskrit : *man* is the
first syllable of *manana* or thinking. *Tra* is from *trana* or
liberation from the *samsara* or phenomenal world. *Mantra
calls thought-freedom forth !* The barrier against it makes a
mantra of it. It will call forth. Shout FUCK and break your

image up. Say all the words that are denied to you and make all deep desired acts that are mortal and have perfect meaning to your meat.

Mantra is a word to break the stable vision when it freezes solid.

After the escape from static representation of man in the arts came a period of great experimentation. The body was ignored, removed-from, twisted, distorted, and great spiritual beauties without human body have been laid down in paint, writing, and music. Now there is a new return to the body with all previously repressed virtues of human lovely beast spirit animal that were uncovered by the experiments incorporated into it. A new vivid completeness enters in the arts with all splashes, drips, and chance and abstract autobiographies of spiritmeat taken whole within a new portrait of man. Without change, that too will become a frozen imagevision of deadmeat.

Outside of our stable visions of ourselves and behind the walls in our spirits is *EVERYTHING*! All unmade acts and generosities and aspirations move there in a tangle, weaving one into the other like vines and briars. Among them are a few actions that would cause suffering but how much more good lies there!! What new virtues men could bring into being if there were no walls and inescapable visions! — What if each vision were stepped through and each image broken? No man can be denied a deep desire or kept from an honest word. Fuck!

Sing fuck. Shout FUCK. Say anything from deep within.

Say FUCK! Say I FUCK! Say FUCK because it is a spirit mantra as is any word that moves and vibrates the chest like a roar. Say any word that returns man to a meaning or names any noble act as vow. Any great swearing. All men are profane and rapturous, wrapped and coiled like one helix inseparable.

FUCK, say FUCK. Say FUCK GOD as a holy prayer.

Those who accept a lifevision or a godvision will not *experience* life or God. And those who deny a word help to freeze up life into a denying form.

FUCK can be an exclamation that clears the senses : FUCK DEATH ! !

My first conscious use of *Fuck* as a mantra to break a barrier that kept me from straight speech and act was in a poem. Wanting a woman I could not have, though she was willing, my repressed desire made my senses blur with smoke of anguish. I was too numb to speak. I wanted to tell her, but she was no longer there. I was smoke-blinded by myself. My desire was not obscene but the frustration of my impulse and my weakness put my want behind a barrier. I sat at a dark desk in unthinking state and stupefied. My urge to love her was lost inside myself. The need to speak to her was strong. Oh Christ oh God oh fucking shit oh shit-shaped pain of love, exploded through my lungs and head and I was released to speak of my state of being. The mantra was a part of me and a speech of my spirit. The line cleared me and gave vent to a whole statement. I was given ease by the mantra. It freed me to give name and words to my feelings.

Say FUCK, say FUCK, say FUCK, say anything that opens to acts.

Is there any more personal creative act than fucking? Fuck does not mean merely the act of copulation but all ramifications, doings, and movements that give sexual delight to the spiritbeast who is lonely and cold and in need of touch and warmth in his separateness. He joins with a woman to make a citadelheavenjungle of conjoined pleasure clearing the accumulated weight from senses. He gives ease and openness by aiding another. Is there a more *personal and creative* gesture? When copulation is unearthly it is fucking. Fuck is the old deep word. *Copulation* and *intercourse* are words made up from a dead language. To have intercourse or to copulate is not to fuck. To fuck is to give moments of ease and warmth to another and to accept the same from a loved one, and to join bodies and clear the spirit of its heaviness. After FUCK-ING we relax. The exalted pair are made more free by their generous act and are in a state of natural ease. They see freshness in one another and in the world.

Fucking is personal and should be spoken of. Men who say *copulate* or *intercourse* feel removed from their bodies. They use those words to create an illusion of objectivity — as if they look down on the doings of beasts. And don't they *fuck*? I would rather fuck with my meat body than have intercourse and watch it with my mind — or pretend that my mind-aloof looks down on a divisible body. I will not amputate myself into pieces that stare at one another and snicker. Fear of fuck is fright of men's desires and liberty.

Fuck is personal and athletic-physical. It is performed by the spiritbody. It is of most importance because it gives new vision and helps clear old visions so that men may pass from life into life. It is our contact with everything and with ourselves and other spiritbeastcreatures. Besides being an action and a mantra *fuck* is a vibrant adjective. It describes a state of matter or a creature that is otherwise without description.

Another stanza of my long poem *Dark Brown* ends with fuck as an adjective : 'BREATHE BRIGHT FUCKING AIR ! ! ! ' Breathe bright fucking air. When the air is splashed with inspiration, when it is radiant and personal and it vibrates, what adjective could be used to describe the state of it? What word is descriptive of great personal act?

It was fucking quiet.

The fucking flower of silence breathes its fucking air.

I was so fucking high I trembled.

Oh fuck, fuck, fuck, shatter me and lift me free.

The night was fucking long.

Oh fuck, oh honest word oh.

FUCK YOU is a vow of anger and detestation. How the word is twisted! But in Dante's Hell the man who made fuck-signs at God — how deeply he felt to make *figs*.

'I will fuck you' is a vow of love and desire. I will *copulate* you? I will *intercourse* you? Or is the man who is a real man never to say *I will fuck you . . .*? Is he to keep his desires secret and tamed and withering behind a wall of censorship and silence? Must he disrespect the desires that make his being? Does a man desire and dream of copulation and inter-course? Or doesn't our sleeping body dream of *Fuck*? Who is the waking man who thinks of *copulation*? Is that man whole — or does he deny himself? The word fuck is sizeless — it matches honest desire in simplicity of statement.

FUCK represents man beating upon what is not contained in himself. FUCK IT! I beat upon it! (It is a metaphor.) FUCK IT: As I beat myself upon another muscled body so I beat upon the world. I beat myself upon the body I love. I beat myself upon the inanimate (— but the inanimate is not lifeless — the metaphor of *fuck* reveals the truth). FUCK IT! FUCK IT! I acknowledge it is real! All FUCKING things are real. FUCK YOU! FUCK ME! I AM FUCKED! I AM FUCKED OUT! This FUCKING thing will never stop! There is no fucking end. *This is the fucking end.* The fucking earth and stars. Blue peaks that fuck the sky at twilight. The sights of solid and untrembling world that enter like a hammer on my clear spirit and fuck me like a solid fire! And how I move in these real things and fuck with them, and fuck them up, and build fine fucking things of them. How I love the fucking world, and long for fucking death to set me free of fucking pain. How I long to fuck all things, to hold all things of beauty and ugliness and make truth of them, and grip them in my fucking hands and brush them with my passing fucking shoulder.

How I long to be strong and FUCK. Fucking is the conscious or mindless beating of body on body, the touching of spirits in order to pass the gift of love from one to the other. All things are living and all things fuck. All men must know that all things fuck and that all men fuck. Oh, do not cast down the desire for FUCK or hide it in the veil and chain of lying censorship and thus dilute your spirit! Fucking is great sexual pleasure, is warm and soft and sleek and silent. Fucking is dear and sweet and nestling. Fucking is personal and silent. Fucking is a mighty roar. FUCK breaks down walls that hold men to a single vision. (Vision is the passage of vision into vision into vision into vision into vision with liberty.) Let no man name words mysteries or make comic laws.

FUCK is the agony of the statement of being fucked and should not be forgotten.

There is no secret language. Jacob Boehme used words to clear mysteries and in his agony yelled and muttered fuck. Aristophanes, before a black and smiling marble curtain, had servant and lord alike say fuck and shit their pants upon the stage. Brahms fucked. Beethoven shouted it in his bulging brows while angel wings of hair trembled on mute ears. Jesus blessed fucking. Buddha knew he was fucked by the world about him. All men who are fathers fuck. All women who are mothers fuck. We see young men think of fucking and old men look back on FUCK.

Billy the Kid bellows from eternity to show his pain: OH GOD, DEATH FUCKING ACHE!

After writing the opening stanzas of the poem I have quoted herein I believed I had inscribed a passing vision in poetry — but with the liberation of language and struggle to free desires I passed to statement of sexuality and wrote the next section and titled it *Fuck Ode*. Then to be free again I wrote the last section titled *A Garland*.

Fuck Ode begins:

THE HUGE FIGURES FUCKING, THE HUGE
FIGURES FUCKING, THE HUGE FIGURES
FUCKING, ON THE CLIFFS, ON THE BANKS IN
THE BLACK RIVER . . .

LETTER TO GEORGE BUCHNER

George Büchner is author of *Wozzeck, Danton's Death* and other plays and writings. He died in exile at the age of 24 years in 1837 — a fighter for political and spiritual freedom.

Dear George,

I've just finished reading your short story about Lenz the mad playwright and ' ape of Goethe '. How much I felt it! How much I felt the story! I have been through a madness like Lenz's — but mine was not so pathological as his. I was without Lenz's fear of the dark and his more irrational fears and compulsions. I, too, was in my own Hell of the inert and cold.

I almost could not finish your tale. My old fear began to seep down on me as I read of Lenz. I pushed the fear back and continued the story and knew that I was completely well . . . I was able to drive it all back and continue.

I am more close to you in my thoughts now than ever before, George Büchner. I think of your magnificent play *Danton's Death* and also of *Wozzeck*. I look to you for warmth as perhaps you looked to Schiller. Or were you in revolt against Schiller? I know nothing of the history of your German literature and thought. I have read *The Death of Wallenstein* by Schiller — I see the greatness in both that play and *Danton's Death*.

I think we are all fated to worship the revolutionary man — whether it is the leader of the French revolution, Danton, who revolts by turning his eyes and will *away* from murder, or Wallenstein the brave soldier who revolts against his liege

in the pride of self. The resemblances of the plays are there
— perhaps it is only their beauty! You must have fought
against the pomposity of the Schillerian verse drama with
your poetic realism of prose. Those literary issues are so minor
compared to the humanity of the two great protagonists,
Wallenstein and Danton. There is so much warmth between
men . . . time cannot divide them.

I have just returned to society — that is what I wrote to
tell you.

My return started this way — I ceased to acknowledge the
demands of society. I quit fighting against the compulsions
and repressions for an instant. The barricade made by my
resentment against demands was breached when I ceased to
force back rage — a clarity of myself and my life poured out
of hidden corners. Now I shall be a man of life and action!
My hermetic life and retirement are over! — It was not quite
that easy! —

The horror and the major fears I had are gone, and I
return to society! How stupid I am that I fumble here and
repeat. But I do return! And I do not accept what I find on
my return. The world is not hopeless and I do not damn it
and pull back within myself to a dream of complete destruction and another universe. That is where I have been — in
a dream of destruction, held by the sight of a universe I
invented and populated with rapine and terror and pale
spinning wolves, cold flames, and the pomposity of spirit's
aggrandizement. But not now — I am done with that!

I have come back through myself not to a society that is
worthless but one that is poisoned. I won't, now that I am
here, condone the poisons. You did not pardon them and I
will not either. The evils around are not to be fled from but
argued against with real flesh bodies.

I've never been here as intensely as I am now. Wait, yes,

I was here this strongly when I was twelve years old and before that. Gradually I retreated year by year, act by act, from the faces of men and women. I did not challenge what I disliked. I weakened and let myself be driven from what I loved! Always within me was a coal of boldness and clear sight of reality, always I could depend on it, but the ember living without nourishing. I was lucky that it didn't expire. I did not develop the coal — I depended on it.

Suddenly, five days ago I realized that I am twelve years old again! Now I may begin to grow to manhood — and with no loss but a gain of extra years that I spent in the strange, and evermore strange, foreign place I inhabited. Now I'm free. Now I'll bring the kernel to full being.

Let me tell you the last things that happened to me in coming back.

I spent two months keeping an intensive journal of all my thoughts and actions and sexuality. I wrote down each petty or important thought and act. Gradually I saw into myself and the simplicity of the hang-ups I live by. Slowly in those two months I beat down the last stages of the blankness that lay on my mind and numbed my actions. I came alive and moved in a larger state than I knew before.

While I worked my deepest fears arose for long moments — I was terrified and made speechless by the look of all living things. When I could not speak I forced myself to make words. I guarded each waking moment to keep myself in motion and activities. If I could not speak when I confronted fear-causing things, then I wrote down in garbled words what I couldn't say out aloud. Later I looked at what I wrote to understand the fear and face it better next time.

I burned almost two years of my poetry because it had the stark face and stare of my fear upon it. I couldn't live with it in my sight. I burned all of my writing for the two last and most ugly years except the few pieces that were an outward call from my life. This is it simply. It was right.

I came out able to act, but I was still alone, still cool, and still in a state of drabness. I occupied myself, but I lived in disinterest. Before I battled constantly to keep off madness and fear of it — much of my energy had been cynical and I condemned all that I could. Now I was without negative energy, the Hell that had been my motivation and reason for living.

I spent a few weeks in that new drab state. I kept myself busy so I would not feel it intensely. I kept hoping for something more and better — then a new tension I hadn't felt before came over me. I lay alone in my sleeping bag before the fireplace. I coiled and uncoiled in my body and spirit. I did not think — or if I did think, it was of an anguish I could not identify. I stared about at empty walls, not wanting to stop the releases I felt. Gradually I realized I was being reborn. I did not know *what* or *how*, and I did not care except to know it was a rebirth. Somehow I had sureness that I would come to life.

When that stopped I knew something more was coming and I waited. I did not know what was to happen — but I felt better.

In the evenings a feeling of beauty and vibrant clarity and simplicity came over me — the feeling resolved into visions or hallucinations of sweet love-creatures in the air about me. I saw with double sight : I saw what lay before my eyes in the half-dark rooms, and at the same time I looked into crevices of my imagination. In the chasms floated sweet faced creatures of love smiling to me. They were microscopic beasts of no-size and at the same time they were large before my eyes.

They had white, looming, and soft faces — and gentle bodies with scales and feathers. They had huge dark eyes, and they sent love to me. They were innocent combinations of tiny eagle and tapeworm and rat and deer. I could see them clearly but could not call them to being at will. They were both a feeling and a sight. I began to change within, to feel love, and to be loved by their simplicity. It was almost nothing.

One evening I drew realizations of the beings — and I wrote the words coming from them. I did not hear them speak the words — but I added them to approximate in some way what the creatures were or meant. The silliness of the words and drawing deserves no apology — I was happy to draw them as I could : *see next page*.

After that night new life came to me. My thoughts were straighter than before. I started a new journal and it was not one of condemnation and self-attack. It was a construction of thoughts and acts that I investigated.

I thought I would die before now and leave one small book of poems. Now I find I have youth and strength and desire to help and make positive action.

I awoke five days ago early in the morning wanting to write my declaration to mankind. I don't know at what instant I accepted the existence of the society about me instead of the inner one that I had made — but I shall stay here where I am now!

So with that realization I write this letter to you.

I believe in the majestic beauty of man and I believe in the simplicity that my senses give evidence of. I believe in a fight for the good that I see and I believe in a condemnation of what is bad for life and mankind. I had retreated from the consciousness of the pains and miseries of others and from the sight of injustice. I had invented reasons (or used my weakness as excuse) not to aid when I could. I had not seen through my prejudices. . . . Now, wherever possible, I will put an end to that.

I think the fact that I finally came through with such ease and by such a simple path proves something. I have no declaration to make — except that I shall seek a declaration of good and push to put it into practice. A new era is at hand and it must be joyfully struggled for in full awareness and enjoyment of life. The change is not only inside of myself. In all men there is a new consciousness. A new combat for freedom and happiness and pleasure is beginning everywhere — I see signs of it in the continents and peoples of the earth. An end can be put to hunger and useless death. I see how many forebears of this newness lie in the past and history. I see it is a constant struggle, and also merely a fresh budding of what is constant.

I have newly dedicated myself to highest poetry and truth without prejudice.

I hope this reaches you through the trails and swirls of time.

Your friend,
Michael

THE MUSHROOM

The mushroom high isn't like any other. All of the hallucinogens — peyote or mescaline, lsd, and psilocybin (the Mexican mushroom) — lift you to an Olympian universe. Everything is timeless, huge, and bright and you're free to walk in it and do what you want to do. Each of the highs is a different continent in the Olympian universe.

Peyote takes you to lands of religiosity and physical matter — you study the physics of light and shade, and matter and space, and color and blackness, and hot and cold. Lsd takes you to another place where you encounter deep psychological mysteries and revelations and mysticism. The mushroom is different. In some ways it is more beautiful than peyote. It opens you up so that you feel internally deep inside, and all around you, the utterly human and humane.

People are the main thing with the mushroom. A friend who was high cried: 'My God, I am a temple!' Then he began talking about Dutch painting and telling me Dutch girls have little stoves of warmth inside them like the paintings do. At moments during the high you believe that everything is prearranged for you to see. The strangest, most grotesque, and most glorious people on earth are selected and paraded in front of you. It's one of the most elevated comic dramas ever seen. All is both comic *funny* and 'Comedy' in the sense that Dante wrote *The Divine Comedy*. You laugh and weep staring at the faces and bodies and weird costumes and godliness and beastliness of mankind.

— A Charlie Parker lp is playing south - of - the - border pieces . . . I remember a girl I saw passing when I'd taken the mushroom. We were sitting in an outdoor restaurant in

North Beach sipping at big crystal glasses of cold wine. We had just had an amazing conversation. My friend told me about a mushroom session he had with people I knew in a faraway city. As he told the story I was there with them. I experienced the beings of each person — one of them during the high had changed into a giant Santa Claus and another had become an Indian chief worrying at the problems of the world. The guy telling me had mentally travelled into the future through wars and blackness, and then new light, and finally to the last crusty day when the earth was a cold cinder. (I was heartsick to hear that there would be more wars.) While he told me the story and about his time-trip I watched him right in front of my eyes turn into a French-Canadian trapper, then a politician, and at last into a great visionary whose eyes were unexplored planets rolling in the sockets of his skull while a lock of Byronic hair drooped onto his brow. I think he glimpsed into the future again as he told me about it. I wanted him to tell me more . . . — But back to the girl. As we left the cave-like void of the restaurant we stopped stone still at the sight of her. Her hips were swinging to some soundless and immortal Parker-like melody that only she could hear. She shook her shoulders and breasts. She shimmied and shook. Her walk was a moving flow of basic sexuality. Seeing her I understood the whole thing — what she was doing and why she did it that way. I knew the biological rhythms, the social causes, the karma, the predispositions, and the final outcome of the strange sex dance that she called walking. It was too much. It was great, *great* in the sense the word can be used to describe immortal works of art, nature, or children and women. Her walking was a work of personal art in moving sculpture of flesh — just as Mozart is a motion in sound waves. It was her piece and she was living it, and she still is somewhere. I was knocked out by HER. She stood out perfectly and solely. Everyone came through to me that way. They showed what they were physically and spiritually — it is all one thing.

Half of the restaurant is under a marquee in the fresh air. The frontmost tables are in the sunlight and flood out over the sidewalk. The other half is a shadowy cave of bricabrac, plaster, and painted concrete. Small ornamental fig trees grow in front. As we sipped the wine (you don't drink much — only for the pleasure of the cold wine) I studied a tree moving in the wind like an animal-creature created out of emerald and bark. The tree was a symbol of perfect love and a bridge between the organic and the inert world.

I was so deep in euphoria that my eyes pressed tightly closed with pleasure — wind-pleasure, sun-pleasure, air-pleasure, human-pleasure. It was so intense that I could not turn to look at the people behind me in the dark pit indoors. Now and then I would sneak a quick look from the corner of my eye. What I saw would break me up in gales of laughter or bring me to tears, or both. I saw PEOPLE'S FACES as they can only be seen with the mushroom, and more than that I saw their hands, and bodies, and their clothing!

It was the first day of the world's creation and ten trillion billion years old, bright, shadowless, and fresh and gleaming: an Oriental city as huggable as a teddy bear is to a child. A dazzling shiplike convertible pulled up to the fig tree. It backed up with infinite grace and deliberation and stopped exactly and perfectly in front of the fireplug. Three strange animals stepped out. The seediest, most grotesque and most beautiful I had ever seen.

A skinny weirdly erotic hustler with long black roots to her hair (I could see every fraction of her physical and mental being), face covered with big sores beneath a layer of makeup, looking like she was going to fall off the thighs of her too thin legs, wearing a fur stole in the heat of afternoon, smiling proudly and girlishly like a goddess she stepped out. *She radiated real shining light beams of joy and happiness to be alive.* She scattered auras of pride in joining herself to the company of the restaurant. She stepped a little to one side to miss the fireplug. IT WAS MONUMENTAL AUDACITY worthy of Homer's singing.

' The best is none too good,' whispered my friend referring to the fireplug scene. I had to bite my thumb to keep from roaring with love. Next, out stepped her companion creatures — two male beasts or gods. People are no longer like our conception of them. They are like godly beasts. Every line, wrinkle, freckle, reflection of color, hidden motivation, and apparent desire stand out in technicolor, on their bodies and faces. Both were wearing sublimely ill-fitting and tailored suits shimmering with freshness and creases. They stopped and stared at all who watched them from the coffee shop. Arabian oils dripped from their harlines onto olive brows. The youngest one smiled his smile of pride, pleasure and joy in life — he also sidestepped the fireplug. As he smiled his lips rolled farther and farther back till scarlet red gums showed over crooked and gleaming white teeth. He stood hands in pockets and radiant — he stared and stared, smiling and smiling — a natural lumbering creature proud to be a male beast. He grinned for another hundred years; we gasped at the drama. The older man also stopped to smile, then he hurried the hustler and friend into the depths to their awaiting table. They were more than stately — they were exquisite, and all eyes were watching them. Homer plucked the lyre for them.

I tried not to watch people. I could only look in small doses or I would exhaust myself with laughing and crying and my attempt to hide it from the waiter.

My friend sat across from me looking down the sidewalk — he prepared me for people coming up the street. He'd say, ' Here comes another ', or ' You won't believe this . . .' All humanity passed us by covered with sores and bandages, and tee shirts, and furs, and psychoses, and raptures — not one of them looked like anything I had ever seen. Every shadow or detail of face, emotion, highlight of lip or hair, or swarthy arm-hair stood out in unique radiance.

All of our notions of the human body's shape are wrong. We think it is a head joined on a torso and sprouting arms and legs and genitals or breasts, but we're wrong. It is more unified than that. It's all one total unity of protoplasm and our ideas of its appearance are too much a matter of habit. The human body and the clothing it chooses are weird and godly — it is often sickening, distorted and crippled. Strangely, it is not any the less beautiful if you can see the whole of it — and the reasons for the grotesquery.

The high lasts six hours and you don't eat. We ordered a sandwich. It looked like it was going to eat us. An escaped tongue of pink pastrami attempted to lap at the plate from slab lips of rye bread. The potato salad came from a dinosaur's dream — a miniature yellow mountain covered with green coral of chopped parsley. Nobody could eat it.

I wanted to see the great show of Chinese art at the Museum while everything was still radiant and timeless. (When we did go later in the afternoon the show was no different than it had been when I saw it days earlier. The landscapes of the Sung dynasty are perfect, immortal and untouchable in their beauty. They are from a marvel world of their own. I heard a long scroll of shark-fin hills as if it were a whistled song. Everyone seeing the show in the gleaming rooms was as high as I was. *They had been turned on by the paintings!* We were at home! I became interested in the tiny figures and houses in the paintings, and in a mysterious wide-eyed Eurasian girl who was looking at them. — I decided to stop stock still in the middle of the show and begin a cosmic and inspired meditation. Everyone will come and sit at my feet I thought — then I will have to protect them from being carried away to a mental institution. I laughed — I had caught myself in a cosmic illusion of grandeur.)

As we stared at the sandwich an old man strutted in. His hair was dyed black with shoe polish and he was mustachioed. He stopped at each table. In mute silence he winked at each customer then smiled and traced 1920's dance gestures in the air with his forefinger and danced robot-like to the next table. His enormous face was contorted with the desire to frighten us, and the simultaneous desire to amuse and assure. He was under almost superhuman strain — it was eerie. We left them.

On the street I stood in the sun, my eyes closed tight with pleasure at the warmth of the sun's rays. I was touched by the new clear beauty of billboards become luminous with hidden meanings and colors freshly arisen to the surface. The whole city was cuddlesome and near enough to touch and caress. I saw the most glorious face I've ever seen on a man — an old newspaper vendor sitting on a little ledge in the doorway of a bar. The dark marble behind him reflected green light. He was a strange pre-Greek deity sitting in a grotto. His forehead was dark brown and his big nose was pink-red and fleshy, the rest of his face was luminous flesh color. He looked at me through steel rimmed glasses and then out on the whole world with primordial compassion.

In the car we drove up and down the hills, heading in the direction of the museum, and talked about Ireland and the Irish earth spirits. We careened up and down hills at thousands of miles an hour in utter timelessness and sunlight. (*Actually were we motionless and was everything taking eternities?*) To amuse myself and to keep from being scared in moments of strain I'd make growling sounds to myself and repeat a little verse by Robert Burns that I'd found in the park. Then I'd say it over again and growl the R's like a lion. At moments the high can be a strain. We talked about what everyone is in the great scheme — one was a faustian man, another was surely an alchemist, another was a visionary . . .

We parked. I'd never been in the church before — it is quietly lovely and designed in part by the old California architect Maybeck. Two doors open from the stone hallway — one into an English garden and the other into a worship room. We went into the room. There is a fireplace at one end and a lectern and stone baptismal font at the other. Large natural tree trunks serve as ceiling beams — it is dim and gray and cool. (A friend saw a photo of it and described it as 'haunted'. He meant haunted by beauty.) I walked up and fingered the bible and stood behind the lectern.

'Did I ever tell you I wrote a play in Beast Language?' I asked my friend.

He said, 'No'.

Then I began to speak in the language of beasts — roaring and growling in that language and I proceeded into a sermon and ended it with a song. Here's a poem I wrote to describe it :

At the altar of the Swedenborgian Church
with tiny white flowers behind me,
delicate in their glass vase — in half darkness.
By stained glass windows
of dream hills and landscapes — I raised back my head
AND SANG
into the Olympian world, growling with the worshipping
and directing voice of Man-Beasts!
GROOOHOOOOR GROOOOOOOR SHARAKTAR
GRAHR GROOOOOOR GREEEER

SHROOOOOOOLOWVEEEEEEEEE.
The white flecks of my spittle
floated like clumps of alyssum in the dimness
of the here, now, eternal, beauteous peace and reality.

Throwing back my head with arms upraised.
Smiling. The blotched ceiling
of redwood became mother of pearl.
And I bowed my head, and I bowed my head,
and my arms dropped.

DRUG NOTES

I. Peyote

Cleaning the buttons is a wild experience.

You twist the knife point at the center of the dried disc of cactus. Suddenly blond silky fur begins to roil from the knife tip. Curls and twists of it fall to the table top. The fur comes out yellow-brown where it is old and dirty, and then the newly uncovered silvery locks tumble out from the heart of the button. (In among the strands are tiny seeds where once there was a white-pink blossom like a daisy.) Next the gray tufts circling the center of the button are picked off. Then you eat the cactus flesh.*

---

* *Lophophora Williamsii* is a small spineless cactus. It is divided radially by a number of ridges. Small gray hair tufts (probably atrophied spines) prickle in circular bands on the dark green flesh. Sometimes peyote grows in a clump, several plants converging on one root or a group of joined roots. I've seen seven plants in one cluster.

Peyote grows around Laredo and southwards into Northern Mexico. Seen from above the plant is circular, a rounded mound peeping an inch or more from the earth. The harvesters clip off the plant at ground level with a sharp spade — the root will grow a top again.

The green buttons are laid in the sun to dry. They shrink and become wrinkled and brown. They peel and become desiccated and irregular in shape, but usually they remain somewhat circular and flat. Finally they look like dried mushrooms or pressed and battered buttons of dark leather.

Sometimes the buttons and roots are eaten green or made into a tea. Five or more dried buttons must be taken — the level of toxicity is extremely low and any number may be eaten.

A mystery of the organic is cast like a benign shadow on the experience to come.

After eating the buttons there usually are two hours of nausea and malaise that precede the high. Peyote smells like a dead wet dog on a cool morning. The taste is not sweet, sour, bitter or salty, but something else — the taste of the universe. The taste is disgusting, frightening, curious, acrid, intriguing and nauseating. The taste and malaise are enough to dissuade most persons from repeated experimenting. Peyote is non-addictive. — As the high comes on, the world of your senses skitters, tilts, and opens to sizeless actuality.

The experience of peyote-high is a physical adventure. It is like climbing a Himalayan mountain. There is a vastness and timeless triumph. Because the peyote high is a *stress drama*, a stress situation, it changes our sight, feeling and thinking. Time ceases to exist. In moments of great tension or stress as the mystics know it, the elaborate and artificial structure of time dissolves and they make contact. Space becomes a *hall of glory* containing casually and invisibly what was once the monumental reality Time. You stand on the snowy summit or the warm steppes of a vision. You have the view of a colossus or a tiny creature of love.

There can be a bad experience of extreme fright and demon-seeing. The baleful and threatening air and Bardo demons of Tibetan mythology come to life. The sight of space and stark reality become vertigo. The feeling of spirituality becomes horror. The air fills with threats and cliffs and chasms darkly opening and closing. Trees loom into unrecognizable living technicolor towers of twisted and sparkling hatred. There is no time and so no conceivable end to the horror. There is no place to run for all is limitless — a voice becomes a tortured concerto of mysterious evil — sounds are hideous music — the sky is orange! This is accompanied by great intellectual and emotional pain — but it is without the anguish that accompanies normal pain. A bad experience is not harmful and need not be feared. It acts as a catharsis.

Usually the peyote high is great. Everyone should think, tho, about repeated and extensive use of peyote — it can cause, depending on flesh and temperament, an almost unending estrangement and alienation and ceaseless visions of nearly unendurable nature. You can spend days or months afterwards walking numbly through life and sitting in a room watching the play of lights upon woodwork.

The high is caused by a number of alkaloids. The most understood and experimented with is mescaline. (A mescaline high is not a peyote high but a specialized high of one alkaloid. Mescaline has been used in psychotherapy but the result is not satisfactory. Rather than temporarily breaking down personality so the patient is more accessible to the therapist, it reinforces the personality as peyote does. Mescaline has fewer grossly physical effects, less nausea. It is more psychic and spiritual and more dreamy than peyote.)

Peyote affects the cellular level of the body. Also it acts on a larger morphological level. It stimulates the nervous systems and jars them to a greater receptivity of impressions and more free transmission of impulses. In addition it acts directly on the sense centers of eyes, ears, touch, etc. It works on the syndromes of physical interior self-perception in throat and stomach and other areas of physical energy that are not centered in specific organs (as known by Kundalini Yogis).

In the midst of the euphoria of sensory excitement the stomach or solar plexus can become *consciousnesses* themselves. — Then there is an additional euphoria of the liberated half-beings of ourselves.

Peyote acts on the most minute of nervous-biological arrangements. It temporarily straightens synaptic chains of memories and confusions and our cyclical repeatings of thoughts and feelings — the hang ups. It creates a revolt against habitual ways of feeling and action and frees us to make direct gestures — we walk straight to our desires without the memories of past failures and denials making a negative cloud of interference. The hand reaches and takes. But there is only desire for necessities.

The smoke of our interior meanings lies on all things. It covers in hazes and wisps that we are not conscious of seeing. Peyote clears all this away and gives the joy of seeing with bright eyesight and ears. When the tendrils are blown away the sight of a graceful pitcher and blue cups on an oilcloth covered table is stark as a vision.

To really see perspective again, suddenly and without a veil, as it truly is is an illumination. As it is normally is WRONG! Perspective drifts and flows and is more horizontal than we know. We have learned to see by a code first invented by Michelangelo and Da Vinci. And to see colors leap into ten trillion unexpected glows and fires and radiances — to see the sharp edges of definition upon all material things, and all things radiating chill or warm light — is to know that you've lived denying and dimly sensing reality through a haze. All things beam inner light and color like a pearl or shell. All men are strange beast-animals with their mysterious histories upon their faces and they stare outward from the walls of their skin — their hair is fur — secretly far beneath all they are animals and know it. Far far underneath the actions they make, their animal actions are still being performed as they walk and smile — and each one so different! There are old wolf men and young fox kings and otter women. They have totems that they do not know. Buildings lean and shake and tremble and the movement of a cloud before the sun changes the colors of air. Dark spaces are secrets. Light is eternity. Breathing is music made in space and it looms like a physical object. Creakings and rustlings are Noh plays. Walls are partitions of space in vast eternity. The crisp edge and light on all things is real and true. Colors are all bright and new in Timelessness.

In the high there are periods when fantasies of great mental weight may be entered into or passed by. A parade of the history of unknown Romes with emperors, and gladitors, and goddesses raising bare arms pass by over your lap with minute sweetness. There are moments of estrangement and coldness when all is strange and unpleasant. Timelessness becomes irreality and nothing exists except the stasis of your loaded senses staring at a scene of meaningless depair. But mostly there is the sureness of looking down on real solid brilliant fact.

Descriptions of the physical appearance of the high man or woman — with reddened face and thin cheeks and lips like an Indian's (this contraction and stiffening of the face is a symptom of peyote intoxication) — and the descriptions of new images of reality, the brain-movies and visions, the oddities of sight and sense as the high comes on or ends, have all been recorded by experimenters. It is all an individual experience of the last degree. With closed eyes I saw the cathedral of the Behemoths — a golden lion the size of a continent rose over the arched door. Vultures the size of seas drifted in the air. There are visions of technicolor geometry of the cosmos radiating and flaring and fluxing. There are visionary trips to real and imagined islands. There are comic visions like kaleidoscope cartoons. White hands speak to you in sign language on a screen of black velvet. Voices echo prophecies in your ears. These brain-movies are endless — all there is to do is close your eyes. Sometimes there are open-eye hallucinations of power and glory, with monster projections of spiritual truths . . . meaningful ospreys and dragons.

The greatest importance of peyote is that it is a spirit experiment beyond conception. There is no objective wisdom to be drawn from peyote though biochemistry shall probably finally treat men with some of these alkaloids. The experiences are not relative but unique and individual and concerned with clarified reality and our freedom in it.

The dissolving of Time and the cosmic super-reality of Space's vast breathing is a vision beyond value for men who can be conscious of Space for only moments in normal lives of earthly seeking.

In the high it is impossible to lie to one's self and simultaneously impossible to be self-critical. All lies and hidden desires of others are apparent. There can be no falseness in such a primal state. Peyote reinforces the personality of the high man and makes positive all definite free knowledge and good aspirations. The high comes upon objective reality as a unity. The new unity is there for man to press himself against anew. It is a challenge that is a love. All is clarified into true clarity or left standing in the mystery of an essential mystery.

Each taking of peyote is a new order and is unrelated to the previous high except by sequence and the resemblance of the sharp feelings and vision. Carrying on a search for understanding from one high to the next is unlikely. But the highs build into a totality.

In an old notebook I find:

I have just been high on peyote for the second time. It was a miserable high of beauty. An esthetic high. Things were as beautiful as bop. I had intended to meet the Dragon of Space, to visualize him. Instead I was only a lion wandering in the mouth of the Dragon. A lovely thing, but a failure. I took twice the number of buttons that I took on my first high but I was unable to cope with them. I vomited like the Indians. I got the whim-whams — no sense trying to describe them. My mouth ran saliva like a fountain. The tears flowed from my eyes. The buttons poured from me. My face was scarlet, eyes swollen shut. After that it was sickness and high. I was left with the beautiful vision of peyote but not the consciousness of space or eradication of time. Also sounds were like strange music.

The Dragon of Space is the consciousness of Space. Who can explain it? To know space extends gray and without mercy in all directions forever. Without mercy does not mean cruel . . .

Lovers are left with the need to explain and pursue the appearance of nature, time and space. You see them as you have always secretly known them to be . . . or as you have seen them in moments of rare sharpness. Nature seen with truer eyes is never again easily taken for granted. A delving into each factuality of being occurs after peyote. (You chase the shadows of simplicity and the everyday twistings and intricacies of sense from the normal.) The accepted blacks and whites of thought and understanding are abandoned. Nothing is taken for granted. Once *high* there is a change forever. The moves of lights and colors upon objects are tested. What are they? *How* are they? The meaning of being a beast and spirit in a universe of objects is constantly at test. No casual or causal laws are accepted so easily after the high.

For some in the high there is a glimpse of a final strangeness and alienation — a complete true sane madness. It is a glimpse seen by many men many times. Physicians who believe mental illness is a disease and not a struggle of the soul and spirit in threat of dissolving are wrong. A man who has seen complete cold fiery-colored emptiness with all of the flashes of lights and radiances and solids in its splendor of shallow chill hollowness carries the sight forever. He cherishes what he can create beyond the emptiness, and he puts what he can into that emptiness to warm it. Finally, perhaps, a deep enough measure of wisdom may come over him so he can love what was always there before his discovery. Perhaps then he may love the things that preceded in existence the new works of his hand and brain.

(I mean to say : A man who has discovered a cold bare universe may begin to warm it, as an artist does the world, and when a man has made enough warmth, or art, he may love again the warm things that preceded his discovery of iciness. But he can not love till he creates warmth enough to feel the old loves.)

Coming upon a sharp and perfect sight of reality a grail-search to explain it must begin. — The old long standing spirit laws of morals, art, and science are destroyed. New or older laws that are found to be true are reinstated. Reality is not as it seemed ! The old truths found out to be falsehoods are abandoned till perhaps they are true again (if ever) ! What does it mean if Time can cease to exist? What does it mean that we have bound up our senses, and that man is a beast of the infinite?

The complexity and richness of peyote dissolves the preconceptions of those who take it. All gratuitous choices, such as taking peyote, are a risk for that is part of life. The risk is that of giving up warm preconceptions for a cold unknown where all must be made anew. I went farther into life and matter than I knew. But it was all truly an extension and intensification of the way I was already going. Later I found fear, horror, and self-blockading but it was of a nature I would have come against regardless — and it is without regret. PRAISE to all things that bring closeness to the Universe !

GAAHHHHHHHH !

Normally mankind sees vibrations and projections of himself on all things. He views through a smoky mist of spiritually, physically, emotionally, tortured and twisted screens.

The screens, the clouds, are actually thrown into the air

and they accumulate. They exist in the nervous connections of the brain and centers of sense throughout the whole body. Peyote draws the projections back to the interior beneath our skins and they dissolve and leave the world vivid. (Once they are cleared away there can be no doubt we literally project them.) Even seated before a table — the silverware, an ashtray, a candle, are a thicket of our fears, past relations, and the suppressed and unfulfilled half-desires that they call to mind. No wonder peyote causes you to go out and to walk with freedom. If the simplicity of a domestic scene is a miniature of oppression, what must the world be? To walk a hundred yards in total freedom is to live forever in eternity — freedom for an instant is beyond measure and is immortality. Huge and free.

Actions begin to follow immediate channels untempered by internal confusions. We see and feel what is happening! A walk from room to room is a 1000 year journey of depth and breadth, not a passage in one dimension. The eye, intellect, imagination, and emotions are free to see Space, and Space is there!

Murkiness is habit. All ideas of science and poetry may be checked against sensory truth. All men can experience truths and judge them. Anguishes holding back clarity disappear when Time dissolves. All things exist in space alone and there is not grief of mortality or consciousness of life's transience.

Sharp divisions between inert and organic disappear. A spectrum and flow of intensities of spirit and life-meanings is visible. The life in 'inert' things is seen and the 'death' in organic things is visible. Falsities tremble and there is esthetic shaking and rapture. The possibilities of Love disappear and become reshaped and re-evident. This can take place in a single high or in a course of years following peyote.

Engagement with the world and air and breath become

possible to any man after peyote. I know that insects are truly BEASTS and individuals and I always knew it. How fresh and real the knowledge returned. The understanding sharpened more than ever before. Always I had known of the life of plants — BUT THE ROSE!! And to see the cold space between myself and men and women — and not to lie of the sight! Oh yes it is there . . . !

AHH, I'LL GO NO FARTHER!

BUT YES, I will . . . Combined with the religious rapture and reveries of great expansion and supersight and hyper-benevolence, there is the eradication of the *thought of the object* that rises between the sight of the object and its meaning to the man who sees and touches. The object, the spoon, is exactly what it is, no more nor less, to hand and eye. It gleams!

There is religiousness — no other word names the height of human feeling that includes the personal and quiet active ecstasy of being a cohesive and singular being within all. There is no barrier between you and what you sense. There is no thought of a spoon. It exists in its most primeval, barest and most vibrant spirit state. It is there to be used, seen, touched or not. There are no inversions of desires — but only the immediate : thirst and hunger and their satisfactions. Water in the mouth is an Ocean moving in the cave of the Universe. We live in a void and we carry the void with us — it is an emptiness that we fill with the traces of our gestures. We warm it and enlarge it or it darkens and closes upon us!

Previously formed hierarchies called *levels of being*, made for convenience in mortal life, pass into nothingness. They turn on their heads and flow one into another and they cease.

It is a titanic state where ideas of proportion and measure-ment, sometimes bringing misery in company with convenience, are gone. (Can real Science be measurement? — Or can measurement be real Science or Art?)

One may walk quietly without shades of self-criticism or fear of emotions like gratitude or humility. Not that gratitude or humility are necessarily false — but there is no threat of them to cast a blight on primal simplicity.

All real things are instant and available. No explanations are needed. All things and emotions are completely themselves alone. It is the view of Herakleitus the philosopher — and it is more too. It goes further than Herakleitus. He could see the melting of all things but not the *blessing* of the flow. He could only see the flow was cold and hot and wet and dry — *but we know so little of what he thought!*

It is the first and last atheist view. This state is triumph of the real coming through the senses. It is a divorce of man from the cast solidity of life and it gives him a chance again that he may marry the life of his days — but as a wedding of his choice.

> *Divorce*
> *Vision*
> *Blessing*

II. Heroin : A Cherub's Tale
for M.L.

Heroin is a mild thing. After shooting it I can barely imagine what draws a man to addiction. But many find it answers needs locked in their muscles and genes. Some junkies seem to have a family weakness or an inherited masochistic genius that leads them to love of heroin. The weakness could be a strength if there were no heroin.

The flash is a tremendous experience — a great physical

cloudy blast in the body — particularly in the head, arms, and chest. It is a sensation of great warmth and swelling. Then there is a swift convulsion of the muscles, and sometimes vomiting that clears away to the pleasantness.

The flash, for me, was not good. A great experience, but not one to seek out. The moment after sent me to write a poem . . . the poem was written and the moment was gone. (Ahh, but wait. The needle came out — I thought I was suffocating and leaned on a table. My chest contracted and expanded, my stomach turned and stopped. Was I dying? Was a huge globe of air in my heart? I had seen bubbles as large as coffee tables go up the fine spike — was I dead? With fear-of-death and with hope I looked into my compadre's face. He laughed at me.) Ever after heroin there is a warmth in the chest that lights up at mention of it.

After the burst of pleasure, a feeling of liberation and bodily exapnsion, there comes a new state, an aftermath. That is the high.

There is no combat with circumstances or events — no boredom or intensity. Sitting on a bed or a trip are the same. There is quiescence even while moving; there is an inviolable stillness of person. You are a warm living stone. In a fast open car you are a herculean vegetable — the wind on your face is a pleasant hand. You half-nod at the passing of scenery. Eating and drinking are the same but without interest. You can feel yourself exist in a place or activity but without feeling of responsibility. There is nothing to drag you. You have *occurred*.

A new kind of self takes over — there is not so much *I*. I is an interference with near-passivity. This is a full large life — there is not much criticism, anything fills it. Rugs are as interesting as a street. Whatever is spoken is as meaningful as any other speech. Life and colors had a distracting sharpness before. You are glad they are toned down. You make a study of yourself and nod on the passage of occurrences — everything is smooth and of the same emotional weight. New correspondences are made, unusual things link with the common ones. There is time to study a face — thoughts are traced on it that you had not seen before. Suddenly you understand an old friend. Time does not bother, painful thoughts are fluffed like a pillow. A hand seems larger while you study it — it has details! Comparing the high to normality, you ask where the daily pains are; they are curious. You sort through them wondering why they are problems. They look different and easy. You take them apart and put them together in new ways — you find a few answers. Eyes and thoughts drift to something else. You go somewhere or you sit. You notice coincidences.

Everything that was held back burst out with the flash and not much is left except a kind of easiness. Life is an unruffled flow of the disrelated. If it bothers, you don't think about it.

Sniffing heroin is different. There is meaning to the popular confusion of narcotics and sexuality.

Usually before sexual pleasure we defy the universe and world. We are swollen and tense with the apparent necessities of life. Often we live in a pervasive anger. Sex sweeps away the defiance and, after sex, in brief but unmeasurable moments there is a universality. There is a realization of tenderness and completedness. Love has been given and garnered . . . body and senses relax into new receptivity. There is a willingness to see and listen and to be heard and touched. Our imaginations drift in the darkness — or into sleep. Or we stand up and move feeling freedom and ease. The bed in darkness is a throne. Predisposed tensions are eased. The still coolness of the world is a quiet adventure.

The pleasure of sniffed heroin is like those moments but more elusive. (How great it must be for those who can't fuck.) It is nearly the same beauty. The high resembles a state of bliss. Both dissolve tight definitions of beauty and allow due and honor to be paid to everything. New ideas and meanings enter. Perhaps this is the *flash* in slow motion. As the pains slip out the new possibilities enter.

There are previously unseen quantities and qualities of life, new perceptions of the daily real and of the body. They are almost undefinable. A loosening of ways of thinking and the visible beauties that things have when we are relaxed. The tastes and sounds of things are more gentle and full and the mind weaves trails around the senses. Meanings of the visible are slightly enlarged. In the happiness water may taste like a liqueur — for an instant there is liqueur in the glass ! — Then it is water again — *how good water is !* Is the matchflame a castle? How solid and still the room is. People talk to you and notice you — they smile and speak.

The common things are sometimes wild. It can do no harm to know them. We bring back awareness with us after sex and after the high. They both open us.

Awareness springs when desires are conceived of and when they are satisfied — and sometimes through the use of drugs.

Satisfaction brings rest and better functioning of the life processes. Heroin gives momentary satisfaction. Conception of desires brings a rush of energy to fill them. Heroin gives you some liberty of imagination and rest to conceive with.

Heroin brings a small physical satisfaction. Even if it is mild, it is unique and true. It brings some rest and if it is not great blissful wholeness-making rest, it is a step toward it. Heroin can light the dullness of life and show there is no drabness except the one we make internally. Outside things are as they have been always — ready to be seen with interest. It could help bring some self-damned men back to their *senses*. (It could only *help*.) Opium was first used in treatment of the insane. Like wheat or air, heroin is an existent combination of chemicals. It should have exactly that importance.

Heroin should be judged by individual experience of it.

Heroin experiences can be memorable if they come in time of need and lend strength or ease. With sniffed heroin there are two states of high. The first follows the sniffing immediately and lasts from two to four hours. That is the state I've just described — like the high after injected heroin, it is subtle. It can be lost or forgotten if necessary duties impose. The high has to be guarded and held to — it does not overcome you or sweep you away to another earth. The world seems to be in a state of calm excitement. The intellect fastens on to the immediate and sees *into* happenings and makes expansions. There is an edge of clearness. Relaxation settles upon everything like a soft cotton blanket. Decisions are keen and amiable — tho if the man high is bothered he may become angry. He wants to hold on to the high.

The second state can come the next day, evening, or after a long period of calmness and rest. It is an even larger relaxation, a good languor — spirit condition becomes keen and there is a restful laziness. It is a definite state. You are making some piercing of apparent reality. New nameless emotions happen and unseen sights come. Reality has a welcome weirdness and is fresh.

On a ship in Hong Kong after sniffing heroin, large profiles of statesmen of eternity appeared. They were benign and sizeless. Strength and beauty dripped from them. The silhouettes of darkness and color gazed at me from their warmth and made a soundless blessing. They smiled quietly with foreign but humane wisdom. I had believed that death by the bomb was at hand and I was seeking some answer in mystic beauty. I was seeking some immortal evasion of death. The smile of the profiles was a strange answer — and I needed it.

Another time with eyes closed. I saw torsos and bodies twisting in air and turning out from me over my brows.

Words of great meaning were spelled before my eyes and rosy lambs moved their legs in darkness. It happened that it was a message of moment and I responded to it in life.

●

A fear of life that is the beginning of insanity, is man's damnation of his internal energies by the part of him that is inert and unfeeling. Sexuality and spirit struggles are at the base of fear. Society will not be confronted with natural desires and hiding them causes a violation and a horror.

The unreleasable energies become more terrible. Men find less and less time to rest, and awareness of complexities grows. Heroin might bring moments of rest to the insane or about-to-become insane.

Heroin is only of importance when men are aided by it or when they suffer from addiction to it. Anything that creates an awareness of the depth and breadth of reality constructs an urge for reality. A man bound up in fear and sickness believes reality is tiny and closes in upon him. Drugs make a brief time when what is ' narrow and constrictive ' can be seen afresh. With luck a new view can be brought back to life and untie the binding.

●

Censorships are instigations of a bigoted and violent few who distrust mankind. Once cruel legislations are begun they grow blindly and lend power to those behind them. Making discovery of a cure a devotion, rather than persecution of addicts, would end all threat of narcotics.

The answer to drugs is cure for addiction — but addiction is damned and kept a mystery by any who can use it as a mystery. Narcotics authorities do not desire cures. The intellectually perverse do not desire cures.

A true warning system regarding addiction could be

established till there is a cure — but it would be useless until the truths of narcotics are admitted.

Glimpses of reality should be open to all men. Gropings for power made by wringing the bodies and spirits of the uninformed should be exposed. A crack of light must be made. There should be no lies. There is not need for tortures. I should not have recourse to heroin if it were legal or illegal, but there must be no blurs or confusions . . .

There should be no mystiques of language, drugs, or sex, or . . . !

III. Cocaine

Cocaine is an *ace of sunlight* that can be snuffed through the nostrils into the brain. For days it lightens the black interiors of the body and lends an ivory cast of sleekness and luminosity to the senses.

I had come from Walden Pond to New York City. In my hand was a new book pressing an oak leaf from Thoreau's hearth. In the dim apartment a friend poured water out of a bronze vial onto my head. The water was from the Ganges. The cold oily rivulets trickled in streams through my hair, and over my eyes, and down my neck. I was very joyful, it was 3.00 in the morning, hot July, in New York City. Perhaps the river water and Thoreau *alone* could have made me divinely high. The cocaine was powdered. (It comes in crystals and must be pulverized.) The mound of powder lay on a round hand mirror so none of it would be lost — even the tiniest grain shows on a mirror. It is so pure a white that it reflects tiny prisms of color. The little circular heap was flattened and divided into triangles. The Ganges still trickled over my scalp as we sniffed the cocaine through short pieces of drinking straw. Each one carefully sniffs a slice of the powder. It is medicinal and acrid. The mucous membrane immediately numbs where it touches — tongue, lip, nose burn for an instant and lose sensation. It takes five minutes to act. The darkness in skull and gut lights up. The cocaine dissolves and slips in moisture to the back of the throat. It burns, then numbs, then cools and leaves a harsh sweet taste. As the high comes, there is a flurry of excitement and speaking and laughter; eyes are bright and clear. It is erotically stimulating. There is friendliness and creativity.

For a week I passed through many states of emotion and intellect. All, all was reality. In the dark of morning by the East River I saw new nature made anew — as in any redwood forest of the West. The city becomes nature. The streets of the lower East Side are pastoral and simple fields of summer haze. Minstrel children and shepherds moved among concrete and cars. I saw through the rat's eyes. Grimy barges and ancient factories leaned into eternity. If it shall be our nature to live this way we must know that Nature is here in a strange garment. Old nature and new blend together into virtues of meaning that we only begin to see. As we realize and feel the depth of it we shall rebel. But see the clarity of its passage! We need not live this way without eyes for it!

Color is enormously vivid. Simple things become elfin still-lifes. A small green plant is the living forest of its leaves, and trunks, and microscopic blossoms. The scent of the moist earth beneath it is a world of scents. The clarity of sounds is scarey. There are reverberations and timbres with all sounds. Pallid pinks, blues and blue grays, the faded paper scraps and heaps of twisted and random rubbish are stark and cold or warm. They work themselves into a vast shifting work of art; men move in it creating it and leave to continue. The wind works it. The seasons toil upon it. The work of art manifests itself in islands that are not related. Space and

Time are different. But it is all part of one melodious totality. Disjointed and sharp but always warm or cool — it is alien, but humanly alien, close to human understanding, just a slight step beyond it.

A green bar of soap with rusty granules is a monumental landscape — there are tiny blues and scarlets in the rust. It is lighted with the light of a tiny universe as the plants are, and as the sounds are. A vibrancy hovers over crimsons. There is intense excitement. Objects and acts still you to feelings. We are characters in a great drama, a romance where the tension of personality is an athletic absolute. A room is a large lighted chamber, truthful in its meanings. A glance to a white ceiling is a book of wonders. All things are perfect. You look for warm colors and tiny objects — they reward you. Everything has luminosity and intent.

Freud was an early experimenter with cocaine. After his initial rapture with it, he denounced it. It is reputed to be addictive psychologically if not physically. The first time I took it I felt an addictive draw; after that I felt none. It is too hard to find to become addictive. The high is not supposed to last long but I found it continued for a day or two always. The high is easy to lose — though you can concentrate on it and pick it up again. With a needle the high probably goes out quicker. Anyone thinking the high is the initial burst of pleasurable energy would find it to be of short length. It brings excitement and spaciousness.

SUICIDE AND DEATH

The man is dreaming of suicide. He lives with nearly constant and almost unconscious thoughts of suicide. At moments the unperceived thought arises to definition and clearly becomes a desire for death. His waking life is a dream. The urge for death has become a part of him. He reacts to the intense pain of his spirit. He is unable to accept pleasures. He does not know that he cannot feel them, and he is unsatisfied by the achievement of false pleasures. His nerves cry out and his erotic energy inside presses against the love-constricted musculature of his body. He hopes to be pricked into release from somewhere on the exterior but he does not clearly know his wish. He causes situations to make himself pain and to stir the human feelings that he cannot feel. He hopes to tear himself open to find relief and to let energy fly outward, to crash into outer walls of repression that are counterparts of his physique-walls. He leans across the table staring down at the pistol in his hand. His arm is outstretched. He stares at the automatic from a tiny distance with dark eyes. He dimly suspects that in the instant between act of suicide and death there will be an utter liberation of desire and imagination; all the held back pain will be freed explosively! For one flash he will LIVE! His life is a role in a play of life and it is unbearable! But can't he grow a new soul and spirit? Shall not all living creatures enjoy
ten trillion touches
and raise their arms into a lover's net
in the mutual surge?
He has but one main cause for his suicide — the exhaustion and disillusion that follow the denial of his sexuality.

Early love is blocked or turned into a mockery of love by authority and government. The urge to fly outward and make experience is dammed and it returns to contort the human physique.

The suicide-dreamer is the sole apprehender of truth and reality that surround him — as is any man. His energy has been withdrawn and he is damned. He cannot perceive reality with relaxed and normal senses. He is idealistic, he has many loves that are stopped and blocked. In moments of clarity he sees reality truly, without the encumbrance of pains that his spirit has accepted. Sometimes he intuits reality, or remembers earlier times of happiness. He is torn — he still sees *old liberty* from his constriction. The others have surrendered and see *no* truth. He is different but he is too anguished to know why he is strange. Normal sights of the real would become grief-causing insanities to other men.

The suicider grows, seeing through an unclosed aperture of senses. He discovers there is not a sharp bar of division between the organic and the inorganic world. Others have accepted substitute-pleasures of 'normalcy' and will not make the discovery he has made. They will avoid it. He saw it one morning when he awoke. At night it is not so apparent, but sometimes in the middle of the night . . .

(Men cannot face the discoveries of the new sciences without threat of insanity. The intense knowledge and vivid awareness that they are constructions of inert matter becoming life — that they are at one with the inert as well as the living — that they become life in building complexities of elements, acids and molecules, enzymes and electric charges — that each particle of self is a divided real-life, or part-life, cohering into an infinity of responses and reactions that are totally free in a massive wave of life — and that all are finally creatures of Meat and Spirit, creates a fear of actual dissolution and meaninglessness. And yet we are something like gods. We *are* truth. The advanced sciences no longer belong to Western Civilization for men can no longer face the truths of science . . .) The suicider came to an intuited glimpse of this and it works on him where others are shielded.

And the self-killer in his partial freedom confronts Democracy! *Do not ideals of democracy cause suicide in the greatest democrats?* How can the suicider acknowledge that all men are equal and bear the heavy hand it lays upon imagination? Obviously it is true! But not for the reasons he is told! He must either believe or disbelieve the false reasons he is given. He is equally wrong to disbelieve a truth or to believe it for false reasons . . . Either is an anguish in life! And how may a young man, beginning to think of suicide, with sealed off energy, whose pains are growing till he canot truly rest, singlehandedly solve the old problems of mankind? Can he state questions that he cannot clearly form, to men who do not care? — There is no aid for him except what he may find in poetry, or art, or science, or suicide.

The repressed love-energies of the man beat against his tied-up and knotted reactive muscles. They try to push outwards. He is confused about the separateness of his being. He feels the energy pushing outward against his skin and muscles from the interior and he imagines *auras* of that energy in the world. He loses track of the obvious visible truth that his skin is his bounds. He misunderstands himself and his *outlines* and he confuses *self* with outward objects, ideas, and persons. Superstition, and degenerate concepts of romantic love, and metaphysics result from the damnation of desires. Reality is blockaded. But the suicider sees clearly enough to discover suddenly and gradually the inherent lies, treacheries and false ideals to which he has committed himself in idealism.

If that is not reason and cause enough for his suicide he becomes cynical. At last, believing he is in an unescapable trap, the desire and respect for philosophy grows in him. This is a last step to suicide. *And why not?* It is utter failure. Philosophy is the belief that truth is something divided from us — instead of the apparent fact that what we sense with opened senses is truth. It is resignation to surrender, apathy, and the amusement of words and categories.

Suicide is the outcome of elaborations of pain as they twine about a multitude of secondary causes following the repression of sexuality. (The senses and view of reality are *partially* closed; there is both aspiration and defeat!)

Let suiciders cast all away and destroy even the possibility of death (of suicide) before their act! (Suicide is an act and even as a self-mercy killing is a gesture; there can be reasons and good causes for it. It can be a realization of love and idealism. The act might be humanely illuminated in its own light and stand as a revelation. Intuitions of the merciful blackness of death are constantly with us. We dream of a sweetness and music to explode into.) But suicide as escape from defeat is surrender to hideous confusions. Men grope blindly and unfeelingly, and stumble without sight into their last act. They feel nothing, and they do not destroy Death.

Destroy it first! Destroy the possibility of *that* escape first — and then decide upon it — and if death is chosen let it be a new invention!

If there must be suicide then invent a *new* Death. Name its real reasons and it will be new. How the suicide is performed does not matter but the truth of why it is done is important to the self-killer and all men.

Let no young man or woman enact suicide except as a gesture of love (not as a *response* to being unloved, which is a confusion of the self with the outside world — a superstition. Love is everywhere, to be given and taken.) Let suicide be a gesture *for* love, for the sake of *pouring love* that fills all. Or let it be a gesture of idealism or highest indescribable despair and performed with clear and lucid mind in full consciousness of the sacrifice. Or let it be admirable grasping for the impossible and evermysterious. Or do it from *inconceivable* pain. To stoop mindlessly and half-aware, without seeing or human feeling, in numbness, to fall, into suicide, is to give up to the causes that should be battled. The causes cannot be battled totally at once by anyone. They are inside of self, having become part of meat and being; and they are outside, in world, in physical acts, ideas, and men. But at the moment of suicide the admission of one single truth or one true act is enough of a beginning to make life again. A single truth or action is the beginning upon which freedom may be built. There is nothing to lose. Life has already been decided against. If suicide is chosen *again* it may be returned to with clarity and consciousness. Then it will be a death and not a blotted disappearance.

Hanging is suicide; death by sleeping pills is suicide; leaping into fire is suicide; falling spreadeagle from heights is suicide; war is suicide; accepting authoritarian demands is suicide; existence without human feelings is suicide; feigned emotions and loves are suicide; cynical impossible demands from self are suicide; self abjection is; self aggrandizement is; passivity is; performing the expected is; becoming a martyr for half-felt ideals is! Suicide is not a *liebes-tod*; it is not an act of immortal life; it is not living but a sacrifice of life. Looking into reality is life; moving in reality is greater; changing reality is the greatest life. Men who conceive of suicide should first try pleasure. Pleasure may lead to freedom and make the death unnecessary — but pleasure is not the illusions that are promoted by the same causes that make desire for death.

High and clear minded suiciders take evil with them by

their deaths. Let him, in full awareness, make some gesture to destroy evil as a recompense to his friends. And if he does not have friends he has not lived and is not clear in mind. Suicide may be generous but usually it is a fumbling away from sensationlessness and from what the hypochondriac calls his madness. Society is not schizophrenic but masochistic. (Men's admission of schizophrenia is a functional symptom of masochism — it beclouds the truth and prevents cure.) Society denies natural pleasures and idealizes substitutes and then denies them to the individual. It causes suffering on mass scale and makes useless heroes to whip and pummel and murder as substitutes for sex.

Masochist society portrays life as being only pleasures so it may give sharpness to the absence of happiness. But life is a struggle of the (physical) spirit. It has moments of both pleasure and agony. It is not a lake of unreachable blandness dotted with fins of ecstatic sharks of intense and desirable perversity. Man's triumph is inherited in his blood and it is built by his arms and legs of soft flesh and tendons. The *unbearable* is lack of Heaven and lack of Hell — that is what the suicider must create life *away from*.

DESTROY DESTROY DESTROY
>   create and
>   never cease. Oh
>   build
>   grand loving arms.

The lie that says that false-pleasures are everything desirable makes debility and debauch and ends in death. Surrender to masochism is hopeless and makes a dull life of suicide. There is too little time for life to give it up lowly. If the false pleasures *were* desirable they are ever unreachable; the only way to achieve them is to please every man walking upon the earth *and that is enchaining and impossible.* Suiciders have tried to please only a few and they die! Many men do not even know that they have something to kill!

The man of pride makes his suicide irrevocable. He leaves no chance of return to life. If he is fully conscious he will perform an act of greatness and generosity preceding his suicide. He will make such a strike against the exterior causes of his self-death that his execution would be unavoidable should he survive his act. Such a gesture would not be terrorism but a sign of love for mankind and humanity. No man has committed suicide because he thought the world was not good enough for him. Sick suicides leave brief and garbled notes of apology for their existence.

The beautiful insane often believe they are controlled by machines and their brains are tapped by secret agencies. To accept the delusions of others because they have genius is a step toward suicide. Even the most spirited men have delusions. Their talents lend appearance of reality to their misunderstandings. The acceptance of another's view of reality is a respect that is a breach of individuality. Respect is dangerous because it is not love. Listen to the insane because they are images of beauty and sense that have become distorted through the same causes that make suicide. Watch the sane because they have grasped more reality and are more free. Imitate no one for that makes false desires that cannot be satisfied, and it does dishonor to the idol. Do not become a suffering hero of the impossible — of masochism.

The pleasure of death is too beckoning and blackly sugary to deny it to the willful, or to any who desire it. But it is impossible to believe that men of will and freedom hurry to death without the chance to make the trial of living, unless they are in circumstances of mighty pressure or pains, or unless their dying is of great aid to some supernormal cause. — Put Heaven and Hell into life before *adieu*.

Who wants to see his living meat become at one with the

world of stones and machines? At one time the Romantic dreamed that death joined him with mysterious dark and craggy cliffs, and vapors, and lovely night. I believe it is a pinprick in interstellar night that we pass through into a vastness of the Negative Universe. There all is music and inconceivable feasting of the calmed drunken spirit — but I believe that fear and blindness blur the passage. Life is here to build into grand soft arms, and it could be and can be, and it is sometimes built by suicide BUT NOT BY STUMBLING INTO SELF-DEATH. I believe that we burst into the universe of Anti-Matter and that the theories of physics shall someday prove it. And I do not know what man can deny the validity of all men's intuitions. Tho the names of the intuition be as wrong as God, or Death, or Negative Universe! Do we not in some way go into cool blackness? And there's no need to see except with the atheist's black joyous sight through the microscope of inter-stellar space and discover thereby that life is huge and warm. Details of old inhuman science become irrelevant.

Before death, dream and act, see good, and clearly see the evils. — Blind flight from life is too terrible.

What happens in the mysterious lives of eel and gyrfalcon?
Daily we devour animals that were alive the day before . . .
*   can we solve that?*

The sheep's life IS suicide.
How much there is to know and cure !?

Inspiration and love of life come about by preparation and chance, and by a strength which is no accident but the outcome of athletic desires.

(I dreamed of thin, black and active figures who are the personifications of athletic desire.)

I've never let myself clearly think of suicide but I felt it growing in me through hated acts and unloved loves. Now I desire to think about suicide and have it ever with me like a strain of music. How good it will be to die! But first I must live!

I would never allow myself to disappear in suicide except to live forever.

Art and the noblest human acts survive. If there is Mercy to be had and given then I want to give it to those who evaporate sideways into nowhere with apology on their tongue, and glaze upon their faces, and senselessness in their fingers! No wonder death seems sometimes to surround us.

The meanings of the old animals are gone!
    . . . look to the Osprey, the Planarian, and the shining
    Salmon!
The lamb is nothing now but a dinner
and the tiger is stuffed.

I have seen cockroaches caressing in sublime gentleness. If we must have cockroaches then look into their eyes at least! Study the deaths as well as the lives of great men. *At least do what you want to do before you die.* I would like to commit suicide for pleasure and come back and sing of what is there. A suicide that does not make you think of the greatness of Beethoven is worthless.

THE MAN IN THE TELEPHONE BOOTH

a footnote on Camus

A friend has given me *The Myth of Sisyphus* by Albert Camus. The friend tells me that I can't write about suicide and death without reading Camus' book. So now I have been through *The Myth of Sisyphus* twice. I read it the second time because I believed that surely it must say *something*. I finally find it does say some things that hold my attention — particularly in the sections on absurd drama and absurd creation. Camus pleases an intelligent and large public because he is an existential philosopher, novelist and journalist in a world whose most concerned members are avowedly or unavowedly existentialists. *I think of Existentialism as a moral ethic and not a philosophy.* Each day most men of honor are confronted with existential decisions. They make an act in a 'godless' universe and accept the responsibility for the gesture. Such decisions are matters of honesty and acknowledgement of the truths evident to the senses.

The Myth of Sisyphus is neither about suicide as it purports to be on its first page, nor is it concerned with death though it constantly acknowledges what Camus calls 'fatality'. It is impossible for me to believe that suicide, life, and death, can be spoken of in any terms except meat and flesh, sexuality, love and intuition. I do not believe that men think rationally or logically about suicide. I believe that men may make such a pretense but it is only to cover the agony of their sexual and spiritual problems — they use circumstances as excuse behind which to hide their true tortures.

What Camus calls the 'Absurd' is constantly being made

more plain to us by science and art. It *is* terrifying. It terrorizes us and drives some men to intellectuality and others to emotionality — not because it is an intrinsically cold or evil or hopeless sight but because we are unprepared for it. We are not ready for it because we have been trained by society and culture to conceive of ourselves as mind and body and not as whole, loving, and godly, human beasts of love and sweetness. Camus perfectly describes a confrontation with the 'Absurd':

> 'Men, too, secrete the inhuman. At certain moments of lucidity, the mechanical aspect of their gestures, their meaningless pantomime makes silly everything that surrounds them. A man is talking on the telephone behind a glass partition: You cannot hear him, but you see his incomprehensible dumb show: you wonder why he is alive. This discomfort in the face of man's own inhumanity, this incalculable tumble before the image of what we are, this "nausea", as a writer of today calls it, is also the absurd.'

Why not acknowledge that this is a portion of the reality of our feelings? It is a vividly clear sight of reality that we are not prepared for! — Keats spoke of the absurdity of Love wearing 'beaver hats'. Yet, who more than Keats accepted? John Keats spoke of a poetic disillusion. — Camus is speaking of something more physical — but both are speaking of clear sights of reality. Society prepares our senses for what they must see and yet the senses will not be trained. They will constantly rebel and the madhouses will fill with the clear sighted.

The most beautiful and potentially beautiful men and women will continue to kill themselves with sleeping pills and with living deaths as long as the wisest of men pretend that suicide and death are problems concerning, or even touched upon, by the intellect and philosophy. — The man in the telephone booth is a creature like a lion — he is furred and he breathes and he has lungs and strange loves that we do not know of! At the zoo we would look more warmly at a caged lion and be thrilled by his foreignness and animality. Yet we do not feel those things about the man in the telephone booth. We have been instructed by repressions of love and curiosity, for which we are not responsible, to know what feelings we may allow to fly outwards to any man or woman.

We are not absurd we are incomplete!

Camus' discussions of philosophers or literary characters, and his insight into the valid truths of the dramatic acting-out of our beliefs, and his concern with whether God exists or not are evasions. They are evasions of the fact that *we* are gods of potential feelings, and warm mammalian creatures of uncountable possibilities. It is time that we begin to create and revolt with gentleness, and demand full life to replace the squinting eyes of repression.

REVOLT

Coming upon some words that begin a writing of mine I was moved by an impulse to write an essay on the meaning of *revolt* and to make an investigation and exploration. The lines that intrigue me are erotic and universal and I mean but to begin with them and to track down one physiological meaning. — The lines are the first stanza of a poem titled *Rant Block*.

For a basic relevant meaning of revolt to us as many-celled meat creatures I seek in a lower phylum of the animal kingdom — the one first to have so many of the characteristics we have. This phylum has as I do 3 layers of flesh : ectoderm or outer skin; endoderm or inner stomach skin; and for the first time on the evolutionary ladder there is the third flesh layer — mesoderm or muscle and organ flesh. This phylum of beasts is the Platyhelminthes, or flat worms; they are at a main branching of many-celled beasts on the tree of evolution. In addition to being the most primitive animals having the 3 meat layers, they are first to be bilaterally symmetrical and to have head and tail at opposite ends of the body.

I pick up here, as an example of revolt, the planaria — an order of small flat black worms with triangular heads that live in icy streams. These tiny spirits move in cold water and seek out the tinier beasts they feed upon — to whom they are *raptors* or dragons of prey. They fall upon these desires of their hunger and swallow them whole, or fasten upon them with their bellymouths and shake them to pieces that they may be ingested in particles through their maw.

These are the first higher beasts. They have the first definite upper and lower surfaces to the body, and the first large eye organs, and complexities of nervous system, and digestion. They are our farthest close-cousins.

The planaria reproduce sexually (hermaphroditically by means of a penis and womb sac with a bisexual hermaphroditic partner) and asexually. I believe a qualitative point in evolution is reached. I say the asexual reproduction should be called revolt. Or, for the image of what I seek, I call the asexual division *revolt*.

The revolt is spectacular. Each sleek planaria creature is divided along its body into subindividuals joined together at the points of division, or revolt. BUT there is no morphological or physiological organic sign of these places of revolt — neither on the outside nor inside of the animal. They are physical spirit divisions of resentment and subindividuality. Simply, there are invisible lines where it is predictable that a revolt may take place and along whch a planaria will divide into two. The individual to the rear grows a new head and organs after the division and swims away. The head end sprouts a new body.

The revolt takes place in this manner : the tail end of the beast tightens itself upon an object in the water, a stone or twig, and vigorously shakes from itself the head end . . . disavowing the domination of the old head that has made all decisions with its brain and eyes. The subindividual, become individual itself, is now headless and self-decisive. In turn the individuals of itself may revolt from the new growing head in their time. AHH !

I wish to make a fantasy as an image . . . the Head which is major receptacle of sensory impressions and sense organs in the higher beasts is most clear at birth or at its first growing, but gradually or quickly it fills with preconception and becomes locked in a vision of the outer world and of itself. The Head makes patterns and *phorms* of the environment and of the filling of its desires in regard to the flowing of circumstances surrounding it. By the nature of its meat these patterns or nervous synapses and chains of synapses become set and less at liberty to make swift change and new decision. The Head finally may act by self-image of itself, by a set and unchanging vision that ignores the demands of its body that follows with its load of less conscious desires and needs and protoplasmic instincts and intuitions. The Head is Chief and the Body follows.

With planaria the Comedy is that gut *and the mouth* belong to the Body — mouth is on the body and not the head. In evolution from this point on the mouth moves up into the Head and together they assert a more single spirit in control of all behind them. Head and Mouth control Gut in evolution after the planaria. But the old body spirits of revolt remain as tiny voices even in mammals.

My fantasy stops. No — here is a little more : the reward for eradication of subindividuals in higher creatures is co-ordination. (More basic beasts can live by randomness and hazard. In times of hunger they shrink, in times of plenty they swell. In dryness and heat they encyst and return to life when there is moisture.) Higher creatures must live with less *chance* in their lives. They must be totally co-ordinated to spring upon their desires that pass with speed *in* Space. They cannot encyst and have second chances. Except for the vertebrates, they have no concept of time. They do not plan. They cannot have argument from darkness within their meat. They must be co-ordinated to leap.

II

At all times revolt is the search for health and naturality. Revolt is a desire to experience normal physiological processes that give pleasure of fullness and expansion. The problems of the earth, or the enactions of life itself, are desire and hunger. The basis of all revolt in one phase or another is sexuality. The Erotic impulse is the impulse to destroy walls and join units together into larger and larger structures. That is the heat of Romance!! To create love structures, the old visions, self-images, *phorms* and patterns must be disavowed or destroyed. Anything that chains life to preconceived goals and preconceived reality must go — they threaten the meat itself.

In society there is a revolt-of-revolt, a hysteria, often more visible (though perhaps not more present) than true revolt. It is nihilistic and dissipative. The man caught up by revolt-of-revolt is either weak in genetic spirit and dominated by circumstance. He makes a hysterical or passionate attempt to take any ANY other path than the one laid for him by society.

Hysteria is a real animal process — the trial of anything, any random activity, as a last meagre chance in the face of imminent death. (*Death* includes a death of the spirit's meaning!) Society has allowed for this random activity in its makeup and has proscribed activities for the revolter who is weak. He is channelled. He is weakened further. He moves into, and fills out, another phorm of society and his fighting spirit dies in dissipation.

Freud, Jung and Reich assert the sexual beginnings of life and of neurosis. Freud is the dark poet of the real and conceptual real. Jung is an anagogic writer who leads out to flight of fantasy and imaginative cohesion of instincts and memories. Freud is like Shelley, Jung is like Keats who makes idylls. Wilhelm Reich is the creator of true romance and a golden medievalist and sexological pioneer of Freud's theories. The value of these men to the individual who is not a psychoanalyst is their greatness as sexologists. In sex lies the complexities of desire, satisfaction, and the meanings of revolt.

Men should be freed, healed and cured, not adjusted. Revolt is a physiological process of seeking. It is an energy state and energy in any form — at rest or in use — is erotic. Without energy the body and soul are dead.

To the Elizabethans the body was the *Bulk*. To men who conceive of a Bulk there is no differentiation between body and Spirit. Bulk performs the actions of the spirit no matter how fine or gross the nature of the gesture.

In the simple black spirits and fleshbulks of our lower cousins there are fewer complications of desire moving to fill need. Sub-Individual revolts from Chief-Head and divides to satisfy his desires. He tears away the head, becomes Chief himself, and grows a new one. It is an act and demonstration of physical-spirit as much as the violent capturing of a microscopic beast that satisfies his hunger. Size does not matter — and does matter! There is no proportion to gauge the intensity of desire.

For the swart flatworm as he moves on his thready cilia and glides on his strang of mucus there is no Time and no Society to act against. The background of his acts is the organization of his body and all the lesser individuals of it . . . It is a smaller universe of clearer beauty and simpler Good and Bad.

Light and seeing are themselves more evident. Degrees of radiance and dark combine with the tellings of fine senses on the eyes and cheeks of the beast. They turn him directly to his desires and flights.

Against the meaning the Head has accumulated and assumed in millions and millions of years are matched the needs of the subspirits darting behind.

III

Fish, Amphibians, Birds, Reptiles and Mammals operate freely in an invention. The invention is Time. Revolt in higher beasts necessitates coordination in Time. Backboned animals deal with time-factors and make intellective arrangements and memory constellations to achieve desires.

Liberty becomes complex. I see liberty as the possibility of constantly achieving new experience without hysteria or fear-caused chance taking. We are more free when love and not fright impells us to experiment. For backboned creatures, greatnesses and hugenesses of beauty and experience are available — newly possible lovelinesses. The Imagination maks us transcendant of Time and we see what is gorgeous. But physically, in the hungerworld, as repayment for coordination, the subspirits of every beastcreature by necessity are sublimated. We must fill hungers within the passage of Time. OH!

The Subindividual in higher animals is not free to revolt. The *being* is Solo Chief — and must be to succeed in Chordate animals.

Revolt in animals living in Time no longer happens by a division of the flesh itself. For success I must remain one piece and whole by the nature of my evolved meat. My revolt must be of complete meat and spirit. I must fight the passing vision within myself that freezes into a cemented way of seeing. I must drive attitude and preconception from myself and remain as close as possible to the freshness of evolved and primal urges.

There is a single SELF now, I know it and feel it. The self is genetic and real. It is not an overlay of patterns of synapses and past actions layered on me by circumstance. The propensities for weakness and strength of action are inherited. They allow for the imprint of circumstance and environment

— but they are a small part of the self. This needs must be and is truly beautiful — a creator of diversity.

Revolt is the striving for *success*. Revolt happens when the mind and body and almost voiceless tiny cries of the tissues rebel against an overlay of unnaturalities frozen into the nervous system.

As a Mammal I must deal with the layering of attitude in myself. There is an accumulation that tends to remain there by inertia. But my spirit calls for freshness of experience and chance to build love. THAT IS THE INTERIOR!

ON THE EXTERIOR — I stride in a Universe of greater choice than the planaria. Because of the complexities the Universe *seems* to impose on me, there is greater necessity for formulations — and they become Attitude. If the formulations remain when the reasons for them are gone I become burdened and live in a vision that has passed. If they heap up within me then there is no freshness of experience and I must revolt.

In addition: I live in Society that willfully and through previous agreement will force on me patterns of existence. Some of these patterns are dissipative and hysterical and are aimed toward the weakening of my spirit. Some are made with good intent. Some are to twine me in love-structures that I may or may not prefer to be joined to.

If my spirit is strong enough to revolt but still filled with fear, I revolt at random and move in panic. I become more weakened and exhausted. Another chainlink is made. Feedback adds to the original weakness till I become bound in an undesirable life . . . i.e. a new but *formalized* pattern of living.

IV

Revolt is a striving to a regimen that is conceived of as athletic and physical. Its function is to uncover and keep alive the natural physical urges of our meat. Some of these processes are sex, desire for awareness, and desire for pleasure. Perhaps they are not divisible but all erotic. There is no need to make instincts or godhoods of them except to divide them or place them together to speak of them. And there is no need for the godhood of the Erotic either, except to give it a passing name. We are free to divide, personify, invent and place all things together as we choose; that is a manifestation of liberty.

A classical division is INTELLECT and BODY! Intellect is a function of the body. But it gives us at moments the usable fantasy that it may stand separate from Body and judge or guide it.

EMOTIONS and DESIRES, like words, are physical parts of the body composed of infinitudes of tissues and nerves and actions of the body-physical.

We are nothing if we are not the sum total of our physique and the history of the actions that we carry with us in body and memory.

FEEDBACK is energy that is not fulfilled and expended completely in a gesture of desire. It is left-over energy washing back in us like a broth that nourishes attitudes and strengthens patterns. The patterns become stronger and cause gestures to be half-hearted and conventional and make more feedback. The new feedback in turn makes the patterns and attitudes of action stronger and the desires are further weakened. They must struggle to show themselves : willessness, faintness and incapability grow in a cyclical process. It is a cycle and it must be broken for liberty.

The Intellect, used as an arbitrary division and joyful

game in regimen *with* the body, can remind us to circumvent or ellipse patterns. In that way it stops the flow of feedback and breaks a cycle of outward actions composing an interior attitude. The use of the Intellect can be athletic and physical as it is a part of the athletic and physical Body. Regimen is a willful use of all forces to achieve an end with economy of exertion. The idea of intellect must be shifting and open to change, and must not itself become an attitude. Definition and personification must change constantly. INTELLECT MUST CHANGE CONSTANTLY AS BODY CHANGES CONSTANTLY, AND THE PICTURE OF BODY MUST CHANGE AS THE BODY CHANGES. Planaria changes as the physical spirit of its protoplasm changes. The intellect must be remembered to be a part of physique.

Body is the major force, and intellect is a contained auxiliary. The body-image is the picture we carry of our bodies; it is self knowledge. The body-picture ideally *is* the Body. But it is not if there are feedback, and images, and methods of action referring to past states that live and direct our gestures. These if they are too strong will stand as a barrier to new and incoming perception. If there are inert functions they must be ellipsed and broken. The breaking is revolt.

The physiological processes of the Body, and the emotions, desires, hungers, organs, nerves, etc. are the Body. And the Body, as in the planaria, *is* SPIRIT.

V

There is no political revolt. All revolt is personal and is against interior attitudes and images or against exterior bindings of Society that constrict and cause pain.

(A ' political ' revolution is a revolt of men against a love-structure that has gone bad. Men join in a common urge to free themselves.)

Memories are constructions of proteins and acids in the nerve cells. They are real particles and constellations of particles. They are not easily wiped from existence. But we are totally free. New experience creates new molecular deposits of memory and makes by abundance a greater 'field' that we may act with. Traumatic memories are best healed by constant increase of experience and rest.

'Your hand by your side is never love' . . . means that if there is not strength enough of spirit in you to raise your hand to me, there is not strength enough of love. Love is noble — and acts! Sentiment, in its worst sense, is dissipation and does not move much.

The regimen and alignment of energy behind an act made to satisfy a desire is revolt when there is a blockade to its achievement.

The man in revolt is outside of everything he doesn't willfully place himself within. He makes a choice of his duration in a place — whether he chooses to be in Society or in a grotto.

Ideally Body-Spirit is in a regimen of revolt and constant creation of fresh vision and *reconstruction* of healthy processes. Men revolt outside in Universe World Air by acts of personal nobility; they refuse themselves as usable articles or objects. They revolt interiorly by destruction of matrixes — and hold with athletic regimen a changing and true-as-possible image of body and love.

BACK TO THE PLANARIA : The head of the planaria from which the subindividual revolts corresponds in higher animals to old images, and chains of synapses that cause attitudes, attitudes whose reasons are defunct. Life becomes inert through apathy — there is interference with the reality our sense organs report. There is an interjection of old knowledge before the body can react to new data of eyes, ears, nose . . . Head in the planaria is equivalent to the interfering processes in the being of the mammal. What Plato said was of great relevance in his day and is now historical and contains beauty and ideal wisdom — but those who apply him totally today are confused. Attitudes deal with the relevant problems of a year ago or two weeks ago or a moment ago — but not the vitalities of the instant. All things must be cherished and used while they are vital, and *remembered* for their loveliness and aid.

The body and outer circumstances change at all instants. We make a picture of the real physique and a *painting* of the real changing Universe is created and kept in constant flux of creation. As we grow, we see more and more what is unchanging. Each action fulfills a vital use or need — otherwise it is a Head or Attitude. The reaction of the Spirit Planaria is simple.

I must be aware of the immediacy of my physique, nerves, and emotions. I do not simply sweep on a tinier beast and go into retreat and safety until it is digested and I'm hungry again. My energy is gladly expended at all times — but I must revolt when energy passes into negations and half-loves that are not fulfillment of my wants. Pride and Nobility are the value of self and self's desires in the face of what would send them slanting.

VI

Aside from metaphysics and psychology there is a SELF and it is strong. I have seen it — it is a good thing to see. Self is the sure filler of needs and desires. Self is the organization of physiological needs that will revolt, the non-hysterical and cohesive force that moves straightly. The self does not acknowledge egocentricity, blind flights or narcissism. He is a solid fact underlying those diversions; they are useless to him and they gratify modified and near worthless desires. The self revolts from the old Head, i.e. the past that lives in us physically in nerves and habits of action and sight. The self resents being used as *object* by others or by circumstance. He is busy with needs, and he revolts. The self, if free, in constant revolt, can choose to be used, or not used, and to use or not use.

The mammal, in awe of Nature, sorts in life and invents anew constantly. Regimen must remind to listen for the tiniest voices of the body. (In moments of great spirit clarity, when I am without buffer, I can feel the ghostlike swift jettings of as-yet-unfelt ideas passing in me.) Listen to the heart, the lungs, the needs for fresh air and rest and the need for withdrawal . . . the need for withdrawal when habits assure that involvement is necessary! That is needed too.

Strength is needed for dis-involvement as well as for open gestures. Regimen and self-questioning are needed instead of self-punishment and dogged filling of unloved duties. Unloved duties turn a living being to an object. Honor of changing love is binding . . . but contracts are not.

Worldly revolt of the individual comes from interior revolts that seek out health and meanings both subtle and gross. There are physical processes so fine we have not yet conceived of them. Organs of sense line the walls of the mesentery-gut and they sing to us with voices we cannot hear without healthy knowing.

METAPHYSICS, in the bad sense, is the denial of what is told us by eyes, stomach, ears and nose. An idea related to metaphysics is this: I start with a truth . . . a beautiful truth of the real world and my seeing of reality. I toil with the truth to draw more beauty from it. I hang solely upon it thinking of nothing else. I push it out and out until it becomes attenuated and strung-out from reality. SUDDENLY the *truth* shatters, splits, divides, into stars and incoherent shapes . . . perhaps shapes of beauty. I am left obsessed with the pieces glimmering darkly at me. There is no way, no way, to put them together into reality again, or even to place them in a line that I may live or feel by. I am torn and disrupted. I have sent energy and feeling into nothingness. I was split from my sense organs.

VII

REVOLT is the constant reformation of the body image until it is exactly Spirit — with regimen and fluxing of intellect and emotions pushing the willful desires to success with sureness and energy.

Fresh physiology of the body is searched out with all intentness and awareness. Patterns of dissipation and hysteria are unlinked in the body. Getting rid of them we must know that the 'unnaturalities' within us are not 'bugs' to be ripped out . . . They are hamperings and blockings of success. They may be eased out and expelled by awareness of deep processes and growing truth of body-image till the picture is more solid and more fine and gross than we dreamed of. Coldly ripping ingrained parts of ourselves away is brutality.

Our senses and intuitions and the tools of science and art lengthening their scope, bring touch of the physical world. Only meeting life gives solidity to the body-image and causes it to conform to the exact shape and verity of the body. Each and every motion is a molding pleasure and a shaping test! Finally we are solidly what we are and we are beautiful.

Regimen is a vigilance and joy. It delivers new virtues; they are in constant state of appearance and disappearance.

We are free to be aware of them and practice them by desire and choice. Each day a hundred Virtues are invented and come into being. A great love, or kiss — can become a virtue. There are natural warm acts heating the universe — those are virtues. There are sights and sounds and smells and acts that are virtues. They are emulated, or die, to be reborn perhaps in future.

There is a high state of being beyond temporal morals, and there is an honor that the free self sees. All of this is physical and of the spirit. Virtues do not serve and they are without reward except for the desire they calm or the successes wrought by them. They are without judgement and are unjudgeable save by the self who makes them. Revolt is without vanity and its pride is demonstrative and transcendental.

Denial of Self by the Universe must be battled both coolly and hotly, and as instantly as possible. It must be done heatedly with as much violence as is necessary, and coolly with a minimum of effort and maximum of direction. Revolt must be made as immediately as possible before the root of a 'pattern' can take grip. It becomes more difficult to act when engaged in inactivities that do not bring rest or strength. The idea of Chivalry is the ability to raise one's hand to a Love and make offer and receipt. If there is no self there is no chivalry.

VIII

The Revolter *chooses* at all times. There is revolt in *apparition* (where a man chooses to be), and in acts, and in the denial of his person as an object for use. *Love* is not an abstraction but gross and fine desires and gifts. How much more it is I do not know yet. A man can be persuaded to true love by acts but he cannot be forced to love by coercion and misrepresentation. Neither coercer nor the *opponent-beloved* have true love. Both of them, like society, become dissipated. Each must raise arms of love. The revolter may withdraw willfully for fulfillment of his true desires or do battle if he choose. Battle is a health and comes from a regimen and investigation that spots *phorms* and listens for lovemeat's needs. Is not all meat Lovemeat?

Regimen of the planaria is direct and without qualm or consideration — like a flower its life IS its tissue and senses. There need be no thought — all voices of organs and desires are heard straightly. There is no moral issue or disruption — there is good, and bad, and need. If there is purpose then need is satisfied. There is strength in the healthy self and no desire for the bad.

We may hear and feel our needs with concentration and relaxation in moments of rest and bliss. The untrue ease of dissipation causes deafness. Metaphysics, denial of self, and attitudes are chimeras. The spirit may rest from its opponents but it cannot *relax away* from them . . . It is also possible to be free by search and discovery of happiness.

IX

A denial of Self may come through giving evil names to what is normal. A normal act named an evil is a depreciation. The self performs acts experimentally — and they are normal experiments for pleasure. Self can insult and bring flowers — both with perfect nobility — but not if either is done through habit or aggrandizement to fill out a role. Self is innocent — unless the *self* performs crimes. (Self does not often commit crimes, and they are the abominable crimes and memorable monstrosities lying on the bridge of civilization.)

Most crimes are *enactments* of roles and are valueless to spirit and self. Planaria do not know of criminality. The free spirit knows crime only as acts of supreme despair. Theft and unnecessary murder are pitiful and poisonous and are crimes of circumstance.

There is no solution in a method of revolt. Revolt can't be practiced by method for it is ever changing. And revolt is no *answer* but a LIFE of the spirit and body.

Revolt necessitates destruction. Revolt must destroy the extraneous if we are to act in freedom. If the irrelevant had been managed and handled then the need for revolt would not accumulate. The self in the spirit becomes weighted with meaninglessness. The self must have a history and the history IS the body — the actions of the body made at all times. But a burdening, exterior burdening, or an interior stiffening of the mammal is confusion and a mire to self. On the inside of the body as at the outside, acts of revolt sort out and destroy when there is weighting and enchainment. The relevant must be kept and the irrelevant discarded. The process is intuitive, natural, and involves chance and randomness and boldness. Experiment must be made. Investment must be disregarded! — investment in acquired false histories of self and projected images that we twist to fill! Investments in histories, and speculations of self, must be destroyed by revolt. An examination of desires must be performed.

Poems, tales, ethics, governments, ghostly loves that are not relevant to the natural physique must be destroyed in extreme. Or they must be pushed beneath the level of relevance. This must be complete so the spirit's aspirations may return to the innocence of its meat-feelings.

Investments become contracts and contracts lead to Politics which is the protection of contracts. Revolt pushes aside politics of the world and the flesh. There can be no politics when revolt is a choice of the self. Those who call *politics* revolt are misguided. Revolt of a group is an agreement not a contract. There is no marriage but agreement — and no duty but love-duty. He who marries duty will deserve divorce — or if he does not deserve it he raises himself above his error with fineness of feeling.

Revolt does not fear to make errors. If it does have that fear it has become an investment in a projected image. The ideal of becoming a human of greatness involves pursuit of changing and flexible regimen — but not the rude battering of a preconceived ladder to power and glory. In all things is delicacy and fineness and beauty, and *with* energy they comprise revolt.

The natural processes only desire complete success . . . they do not ask for a permanent insurance which is false ease. Revolt establishes a way of life but does not take out revolt-insurance on the gain. The gain of life must pass and be changing or it is attitude. The planaria that revolts carries within itself its future revolutions.

My spirit does not invest in any thing, object, or idea, outside of me. There is nothing that I know will be forever of vital interest. All outward things change as all inward things. *It is not relative* — but it is the surge of life!

Revolt in its enactment passes through many frozen ways of seeing. Visions through which revolt passes are physical, erotic, and circumstantial. (My senses and intellect revolted violently in sheaths of horror and loveliness and desire for godhood; my bodyspirit diverged from them in a chemical and physical way and remined inert and dissipative. To the outer world I was brunted and blurred.) There are many third states besides revolt and dissipation; they too must be recognized and named and understood and allowed to shift, change and live.

When the time for revolt comes, the states of inertia are studied and judged against. Other states are adjudged healths, or simple and innocent parts of the body and its history. How cold that sounds! . . . am I wrong? There is actually no blotting away of history or of act or action — but some things must be remembered and put from mind. Some must be held constantly in thought for the shape of what they represent. Health is not a constant state :

> *In athletes a perfect condition at highest pitch is treacherous. Such conditions cannot remain the same or be at rest. Change for the better being impossible, the only possible change is for the worse. For this reason it is an advantage to reduce the peak condition quickly, in order that the body may make a fresh beginning of growth.*

So Hippocrates, father of medicine, recommends the destruction even of health for the end of greater health. He recommends that investments be destroyed. He suggests that physical perfection is an aspiration that must be put aside before it freezes into debility.

X

It is raining and two lovely women come into the room with drops of water on their cheeks and hair. They are like flowers. Their faces are flushed. Through the walls I feel projections of rain tho I cannot hear it, it is too quiet for that. Perhaps I feel vibrations of moss upon the wall as it opens to life in the wetness. Perhaps the flat black worms, the dragons of sizeless tinyness, feel the growing of the great green plants about them as I faintly feel the rain and the lives that come with the rain.

(The sexual vision of my poem *Dark Brown* is a revolt I pass through. The last section of it is a revolt against a vision and a return to mimesis of the real.) Revolts do not freeze but continue as revolt. Revolt is easy — and not easy; it is not a gift but health that can be given by no one. It is the self's marshalling and division and concentration of forces seeking fresh reality. We live in the visions of men and pass through them as they passed. We live in the midst of spirit-inventions of men and women. The Inventions and Visions that they have created and torn open are signs to us of courage and desire. Lovers are highpoints of history. Desire is not mortal but moves on forever. The Universe is cold and warm with heats of energy in it. The heats are sizeless as the universe for there is no scale to apply. There is no Cynicism that may stand in judgement. Revolt pushes to life — it is the degree farthest from death. Stones do not revolt. There are no answers. Acts and violence with cause are sweet destruction. And the sadness that there must be any death. There is no plan to follow. All is liberty. There are physical voices and the Voice of Meatspirit speaking. There are physical voices of the dead and the inert speaking. The dead is the non-vital past that lives within us and about us. There is liberty of choice, and there is, or is not, a greater Liberty beyond this. But there is constantly revolt and regimen of freshness.

— for Keera and Susie

ARTAUD : PEACE CHIEF

In his great radio broadcast *To Have Done With The Judgement Of God*, Antonin Artaud tells a constant message that our consciousness seeks to bring us. — It is the message of the *pain of space* and the *space of pain* within us . . . that we are physiologically being crushed and exploded by our own organs*, and by insane aspects of society, and by the vacuous presence of normal space that horrifies and revolts us in moments of extreme anxiety as it calls its love to the molecular level of our consciousness. Joyous sexual love and mammalian ebullience, our motives for being, go wild and die when we admit the horror of another love song — the *lieder* of molecules and space amongst which we exist as another type of being. This is much to believe but the more we read Artaud the more we admit what he is speaking about. *Is it better left unsaid?*

Artaud has converted the *inhuman* to the beauty of Man. If he had not made this speech then perhaps civilization would not survive. Artaud is more than a man of literature. He has turned his body into an instrument of science and become a being of history. The U.S.A. is a spangled and glorious, lovable and terrible culture teeteringly balanced on an ancient continent . . . that is a truth and a physical metaphor for the bodies of Men. We wish to be only *fresh and new* beauteous beings — and *we are !* But certain things have been left unsaid — Artaud has said them.

Hidden fears of reality that lie within men have come to

---

* That we have become abnormal parts of nature seeking strange ways of relief.

the surface in *To Have Done With The Judgement Of God*. Milton has said them in *Paradise Lost* and Dante has shown them in *Paradiso*. Never before have they been said with so little pretext. There is an unadmitted science that we must incorporate. We, new creatures, must accept the admissions of Artaud and tantric Shakti texts such as *The Serpent Power* and all images of reality and body. We need not be afraid. Artaud has become a peace chief battling against the unspoken so that we may have peace . . . we may be ourselves.

I believed *To Have Done With The Judgement Of God* was a vision and parable. I likened it to *Visions Of The Daughters Of Albion* by William Blake. Now I don't think it is vision or parable. It is the most intelligent book of recent times. Past the thin veil of Artaud's occasional madness is the utter and true individual glimpse of reality. It is the sight of reality of a consciousness wishing to be disembodied (because of its horror of physical being and the corresponding view that our liberties are directed by our organic physicality). Artaud disavows all that is flesh and excrement — all that we are and produce. The broadcast is like The Sermon On The Mount. It speaks in real terms but its meaning is so subtle and brilliant that it seems elusive and demands belief in an act of understanding. Artaud the man, and his face, are stamped on the pages. The book *is* Artaud and his screams reverberate to make peace.

DEFENSE OF JAYNE MANSFIELD

This essay was written before the death of Marilyn Monroe the Perfect Mammal — and I send her my farewell in another book . . .

Jayne Mansfield is a member of a black American tradition that stretches from Poe to her — and includes Thoreau and many known and unremembered beings.

There's no more contrivance to Jayne Mansfield than there is to Thoreau or Poe. I'm not speaking of her art as actress. I speak of her as a being. Thoreau and Poe are similar creatures — they capture human imagination by their *existence*. That they catch thought doesn't mean they are synthetic or contrived. I think the three have a secret darkness in common.

I only think of her physical beauty. With Poe we speak of the beauty of his physical mind, and with Thoreau we think of the physiology of his desire for freedom.

A blackness and sexuality and mystery cloudily surrounds all lambs of this world — there is an intense secrecy beneath everything soft. This is not purely an American thing — tho we see much of it here — there is an alienation of creature from creature on our continent, and it fosters mysteries. The great French poet Antonin Artaud is one of the lambs of Europe.

There is nothing more synthetic in the body of Jayne Mansfield than there is in the writing or brain of Artaud. Artaud is a warchief of history as well as a lamb. Artaud is as real a warchief as Crazy Horse and Jayne Mansfield is as much a black lamb as Artaud. Artaud fought for eternal truth and beauty and the immortality of his super-masochistic soul. We only dimly know and faintly guess for what Crazy Horse died — his mind is a foreign universe forever closed. (What sight of American mountains and Bison did he envision over Custer's corpse?) I know that Artaud is a lamb and a warchief and I know Jayne Mansfield is at least a lamb. My eyes and body tell me she is a lamb. If she were contrived her capturing of my love would be more strange. In the dark tradition it is possible that the most sure members are not conscious of the mystery they carry in their physique or words.

The tradition of blackness is a heritage of health carried unconsciously by innocents. The darkness is *Love* that is driven undercover into their bodies or souls and spirits. It makes them darkly luminous. They are the carriers of a lost and necessary health that is desired by those they attract. The innocents, the lambs, that carry darkness must be understood and loved!

Poe, Thoreau, Mansfield are trappers of men's imaginations — whether they do it by bodies of words on the page or by lovely gestures.

How does the lover of every spring flower, awaiting the specific day of each blossoming, become driven to write on civil disobedience? How does a poet of such fine sensibility as Poe's become involved with the music of decay? His sensibility is lamblike. (Read *The Narrative Of A. Gordon Pym*.) Poe's love of clarity and science fastened on more than the decor of love-of-death; his secret writings are a view of the universe that he came to by inspired and idealistic thought. The true-black that lies unnoticed in so many beings is healthiness and a striving for health — it is the desire to see, be, speak, and disobey.

The importance of a work of art notwithstanding (Jayne Mansfield leaves no works of art), there is a great importance to each dark being.

Marlon Brando is singular, but he does not contain blackness. He enacted the desire to act and we trembled. Brando and Jayne Mansfield are both temporal — and Artaud, Poe, Thoreau are immortal. All of them cause us to tremble. There are always overlappings of mortality and immortality, and art and being and being and art . . . it cannot be unraveled because it need not be. There's a secret : *we are all creatures of talents and qualities* — some humans attract our imaginations because of a darkness that they glow outwards, and we long for it.

Jayne Mansfield draws by the black mystery of her physical presence. I know it is a soundness and a wholesomeness I see in her and I admire it. It is strange that men put down her health — it is so mysterious and dark because it is rare, and more so because it is suppressed by most who have it.

Surely most loving men would want Jayne Mansfield's love. In Latin America crowds shout for the sight of her breasts, and she shows herself.

Jayne Mansfield is ambitious — how black and simple and lovely her ambitions are. How straight she must be with herself sometimes ! She looks so sane ! There's something clean and simple about ambition — about having your body and winning with it.

The artist may be a catalyst but how can he work, what may he work with, without the sight of the talents and qualities of men and women? How few show themselves as simply as Jayne Mansfield. Perhaps all suppressions are related — and much beauty is a luminescence of the darkly unseen. But that is not a reason to hide — it is a reason to bring to light — there will always be a new beauty recoverable ! Where are the bones of Crazy Horse?

Jayne Mansfield's secret and her darkness and her wholesomeness are her sexuality. Thoreau's mystery was his health too — his desire to expand and disobey and withdraw at the pleasure of his own dilation and longings. Thoreau and Mansfield are dark because both must hold within what they should be free to display — it is only dark because it is undercover. The abundance of darkness manifests itself upon the face of Mansfield and the pages of H. D. Thoreau. What mass of Thoreau's thoughts and feelings are left unsaid? . . . What he didn't say is nearly apparent.

Darkness is upon Jayne Mansfield's face and her arms and fingers. Even there she must hold back to pass censors and creators of suppression. Sexuality is plainly black and mysterious in itself. Sex in darkness and sex in light is always black. We live in an age that darkens sex and often brings hunger to the fields of plenty.

The Greeks, responding to the universe, were lovers of sleek and firm flesh — it was at hand for them — for eye, for touches, for kisses and garlands. They loved exaggeration of sexuality — they consecrated temples to the breasts and buttocks of Venus. They loved the supernaturality of huge breasts and they were intent on the loveliness of buttocks. They would believe that the torso and limbs and smile of Jayne Mansfield are supernatural.

If Jayne Mansfield's body is Spirit, and I think that it is true of all, then she is supernatural! Her breasts and beauty and body are to be admired. Jayne Mansfield and all lovely sexual beings are held back to a half-sexuality and they may not achieve completed voluptuousness. There is health in her that is half-manifested — but that is not her fault; *she tries.* She is blocked from completion and fullfillment.

Athens would worship her as Buenos Aires did — or more, Athens would make statues of her.

The secret and mystery of Jayne Mansfield is apparent to the puritanic — the blackness is obvious. She wears the black fur of her body and is crowned by whiteness.

The fame that she has is accounted to the shameless wet-mouthedness of her beauty — but I mean that too . . . it's part of her mystery and supernaturality . . . the blackness of her health catches at us in our dreams.

Give Jayne Mansfield roses and lilies, and rare honey and juice of apricots and liquors more secret than drambuie and the whitest most perfect bread. Let Anacreon praise her, and the scholars in two thousand years shall argue whether the verses are silver or golden. She is a dark creature — let the words that come from her lips be remembered; perhaps if she is *cherished* then words of unearthly wisdom will accompany her beauty. We must not imagine what she is or expect what she is. Leave her to BE and show us her supernaturality.

Free Jayne Mansfield and let her wholly manifest herself! What may she show us of love? — she who is by exaggeration of body and spirit so much a creature of love!

That which is beautiful is not synthetic tho it must sometimes come out on a field of falseness — she was borne into it by her body. Let the darkness out to the light . . .

II. MANSFIELD & HARLOW
Oh, lamb, lamb, could I but remember
the poem I wrote for you
in the book that now lies burnt.

Jean Harlow I didn't destroy the poem I wrote for you. And you don't need a defense.

Jayne Mansfield you are THE BLACK. Jean Harlow you are *La Plus Blanche* — the most white. Marilyn Monroe is THE MAMMAL. Jayne Mansfield alone needs protection and a champion — but you are all creatures of love.

Jean Harlow, were you a better actress than Mansfield or Monroe? . . . I only saw you twice. Once in a film you stepped between Laurel and Hardy in a hotel lobby — you glided between the thick and thin of comedy like a woman of velvet between two shadows. I was stirred as they were — and they didn't put it on. I saw part of CHINA DOLL —

I couldn't watch it, even for your sake, or *for* your sake I wouldn't watch it. But I hoarded pictures of you . . . they are locked tight in my brain. I have never found a biography of you (— nor of Lana Turner, tho I've read her love letters in the newspapers and they should be printed as a tribute to the warmth of women.) I don't care if you could act or not. I fell in love with you in a half minute — your greatness of being brings about love. Some see you as tough whore or nymph — but they see you with the same eyes. You are a unity !

●

I wrote the poem with a still of her profile before me, but it was not her face that caused me to feel loveliness — the sight of her walking came to my eyes. When she stepped Jean Harlow did not touch the earth — but she did touch it — and she didn't pretend that her toes were not there on it. She passed by with liquid sexual grace of a woman. She didn't take the grace-pose an actress makes before the camera for a million million admirers in futurity. She moved and smiled with the whiteness of life, and she turned to stare ! The still photo pictures only her face and a sensitive sleekness to eye, to chin and to gaze — and a yearning in her neck and shoulder.

A poem I wrote for Jayne Mansfield, and burned, was caused by a photo I saw of her. She lay naked with a towel over her buttocks. She looked up smiling her lovely smile of huge lips and white teeth. Her enormity and supernaturality stretched out upon the boardwalk like a mysterious fleshly first-aid kit of love . . . She had some good thing that was badly needed and she gave it freely. It seemed that what she had — her medicine — was more than aid; it must also be a challenge. To love Jayne Mansfield would be to find the super-normal in yourself — to reply to her love. And is not that supernormal a true norm ? She seems like a red-cross lamb of love with darkness gleaming through delicacy, slim arms, and huge bosoms, into the sunlight. In another snapshot she holds a tiny teddy bear to her breasts — its nose presses through the opening of a transparent negligee to her nipples — while she looks down smiling with her platinum hair piled up on her head like a waif. And I've seen stranger pictures too. I like her eyes. I always wonder what she *might* do in life — if she were free to do it. What public demonstration or celebration of love would she make from her blackness if she were free to do it?

Jean Harlow is the whole moist woman and white beast — she seems only to bring simple love — she is sophisticated and the love is still simple — she wants to bring and receive pleasure with pointed highlights of emotion. Though one is black and one is white, neither Mansfield nor Harlow would injure or tear at a lover. Jean Harlow makes no challenge — she asks for a partner and protector, and though her body is spiritual she longs with a soul we all understand. The breasts and vast smile of Jayne Mansfield are a meat-spirit that we can barely conceive of.

The sight of Jean Harlow, womanly and striding, makes gentle concussions that become immortal statuaries in the memory. The appearance of Jayne Mansfield is a sexual occasion. She does not disguise the event, she makes it for us. She does all that can be done with an instant of speech or photograph — sexuality flows from her in undulant and almost comic fullness and implies what is still there. She seems to mock herself with good humor and surplus. It is wrong to think the dark tradition is without humor or full of gloom — Poe is one of the comic writers . . . even *Walden* has humorous passages. And why is Mark Twain immortal?

Would a small child seeing Jean Harlow in a film remember? Or would he think, in his simpler world, that all women are like Harlow — or that they should be. Jean Harlow has a gift of common and almost perfect love — there is nothing *unattainable* in her. She has a shadowiness — but it is the darkness of a comedy that depends on a higher vision of her soul — her sexuality is white and simple and not dark. Harlow has no *demand* or ecstasy of the flesh — but she searches for feeling and has a gift of intense and gentle pleasure. I think a child *might* remember Mansfield more . . . in the night.

Perhaps Harlow is most to the man or youth who has suffered from love.

And there is Marilyn Monroe who is a classical balance of men's desires; she is the most understandable for she contains all — she is no specialist but a perfection — she is understood at once but the understanding is not casual. Monroe is neither black nor white — she's rosy.

Harlow shows the simple greatness of women — she is an embodiment of simplicity and flow of pleasure. There are more beautiful *eyes* than Harlow's — but there is no more beautiful creature.

Mansfield brings to memory faces and bodies of childlike challenging sexual ecstasy. But should it be challenge? Harlow makes me think of tender pleasures without threat. There are huger breasts than Jayne Mansfield's — but there are few beings like her, and the others hide their Blackness behind a cold face.

Let us give honor to beauty in all beings and set men and women free so they may make their secret selves apparent. Let's not block Jayne Mansfield's unmade acts of sexual and voluptuous greatness, nor any other creature's. What would be the fulfillment of any person's qualities and talents? The Greeks were wise with their beauties and praised supernaturality and naturality alike — and loved women's flesh. Let all beauty be named and recognized as beauty.

A Lover would not deny the blackness of Jayne Mansfield — even tho he prefers his own madonna. To deny is to cancel a part of what love may be. I'm tired of voices of definition and denial.

The dark quality of Mansfield in each being should be cherished — even when there is only a trace — and she flows with it. Harlow and her quality are loved. We will carry Jean Harlow into Space, and Mansfield is still among us. For truth there must be liberty of all loves.

> Man, free thinker, are you really solitary, reasoning
> On earth where life shakes everything?
> Your liberty is disposal of your forces
> But the Universe is absent from your resolutions.
>
> Respect an active spirit in the beast.
> Each flower is a spirit-genius locked to Nature.
> A love mystery lives in metal.
> All is sensate! And everything is mighty on your being.
>
> Beware in the blind wall a prying stare.
> Matter is equipped with a voice!
> — Don't make it serve a single impious use!
>
> Often in a dark being lives a hidden god.
> And like a newborn eye, covered by lids,
> A pure spirit rises under the skin of stones.
>
> — Gerard de Nerval

An eternal love-shot lies in all that's modern, and the hallucinations of pure beauty are as sizeless as a universe. Man and woman and child know their loves and hungers, and the irises and constellations are one thing. Cuba, and anger, and gold will not change or become less warm by lies.

Blackness, sexuality and freedom must not be denied in any shape — or they wither. Love and the Mysterious knock at the door! To deny any beauty is to deny a part of liberty — but everyone is free to do that. To deny any beauty is to deny a part of truth AND ALL DARK WHITE LOVELINESS!

REFLECTIONS AFTER A POEM

He who has faced the sun steodily
Believes he sees, before his eyes, flying obstinately
All above him, in the air, a livid spot.

Even so, all young and even more audacious,
I dared fix my eyes one instant toward a glory :
A black point is settled on my avid eye.

Since then, mixed with everything like a sign of gloom,
Throughout, on each spot which stops my eye,
I see it poised also, the black spot !

What, always ! Between me and happiness forever?
Oh ! No one but the she-eagle — bad hour for us ! Bad hour !
Beholds the sun and glory with impunity.

— *The Black Spot*, by Gerard de Nerval

LET US THROW OUT THE WORD *MAN*! Such poems as this translation of Nerval remind me that I am a MAMMAL ! We have almost worn out the word *man*. This is the young creature looking into the world. The poem makes me see the surge of life. The word MAN is not romantic enough ! Nerval is showing us our kinship with all creatures. We feel close to all living creatures here . . . but we feel the most close and the most joined with the warm blooded. We cannot know the universal and philosophical consciousness of deep sea animals. We fill the universe in our sympathy for all being, but moments of extreme vision and beauty swell us out so that we feel immediately more related to a larger group than Man. We become Mammals as we were once Men. After such poems, or sights of nature and art, only the more romantic word can have meaning. (Ornette Coleman is a mammal, the snow leopard is a mammal, Schubert is a mammal. When we look to birds for symbols we find the falcons and eagles because they are the most warm blooded and mammal-like of birds. When we look to fish and sea creatures we take up the salmon and kraken — the most warm tempered!)

— I wish I could make a broad silk banner with all of the full, warm feelings and acts of mammalian possibility being enacted by all mammals in technicolor upon it.

The poem enlarges the universe. A new cranny has been looked into and we find we are in a larger place.

When we do not see ourselves as the typed thing *man* we are capable of Nervalian revelations and extensions of consciousness. Then our abilities to explore life are less impeded. Let us be the fullest thing it is possible to be.

It is ourselves that bring the universe to life. We bring it to the life that we know. We pour our consciousness into it and make it a good place. — Those furred and bearded lion men of the circuses and freak shows, by their beauty, show the fact that we are torsos and organs of blood and feeling. This is exactly what Nerval does.

I can't help but see men and women wearing invisible manes as they stride the streets holding the hands of their cubs. I do not want to see them as the cold creatures that they pretend.

This is a subtle experience that Nerval has had. (The black spot reminds me of descriptions of ether-sniffing. As you breathe in the fumes a black spot races at you like speeding locomotive swiftly becoming larger and larger till it encompasses you and you are *out*. Also I wonder if the black dot may not be Nerval's sensing of the *macula lutea*, the dot on the retina that has the thickest grouping of cones whereon the most vivid visual impressions register?) I don't mean that the 'spot' is the most subtle of experiences, but Nerval's statement of it and what he makes of its meaning is rich and glorious. I sense real aspiring animal truth. The poem represents a whole state of mind, beauty, and being — the awakened creature!

There's a photo I like. It is a monumental and 'mammalian' landscape — a blowup of cube crystals of rocksalt on a craggy yet warm landscape. When I see the picture I think: 'Beautiful creatures could live there in that surrealist and yet so warm landscape — it is a place for warm blooded creatures to inhabit.' Nerval's poem opens the same landscape of feeling.

The poem reminds me of the Ink Splash Scroll of the painter Sesshu. (The Japanese painter of the 15th century.) Aside from being a black dot itself, Sesshu's masterpiece is another bizarre landscape that calls for warm humans to come and live and love in it and be awakened.

When I first found Nerval's poem I began a series of paintings of black spots. (I painted them in gleaming blue-black.) I splashed and dripped the shining enamel in large patches. I was looking for meaning. Simple and clear images passed in my mind. Finally I saw and felt that Nerval must have — it's all there in his poem. I made my own mammalian extensions on his lines.

The lines of Nerval are not sorrowful but magnificent. They call to mind the beauty of gyrfalcons — the large northern bird of prey. (Once they were used as ransom for a king held in the hands of Saracens.) The gyrfalcon is the most mammal-like and warm blooded of birds . . . It is the most intelligent in wit, humor, and love. The gyrfalcon stares at us from another dimension with proud eyes aloof and full of curiosity, love of life and depth. The gyrfalcon (huge hunting creature of brainy muscle) is *guapa*. Nerval's poem has the same size and eloquence as the stare of a gyrfalcon peering from a falconer's wrist. The poem is not of sadness but of the most aspiring reality.

What greater thing is there than to fill out the fullness of being a mammal? And to know that these almost other-dimensional awarenesses seen by Nerval are without end . . . And isn't the black spot a woman?

REASON

I

A man lies in sunlight on the floor. His eyes are closed. He does a yogic exercise of spontaneous stretching and muscle flexing. His body demands it. All he feels is a large blackness inside of head and body and the pleasure of the exercise. If his eyes were not already closed the pleasure would shut them. He requires a liberty he does not receive in the normal processes of living. He groans, writhes, twists, denies himself nothing that the sinew and tendons and lung and heart request. He has allowed his consciousness to become a blank field. Occasionally a question moves across it. He wonders how long he has been there enacting a primary satisfaction for the muscles. He knows it is not long enough and the question recedes. There is a passage of time but measurement has ceased and there are only the muscles enacting themselves and creating shapes and motions that they have been forbidden in daily life. He throws one leg across the other and rolls his hip — he repeats with the other leg and then with the opposite leg again, over and over. A rhythm is established. He flexes his arms and he growls. He stretches his leg and his arm, and he flexes and growls another sound. He repeats it endlessly. The muscles make variations upon the pattern they create in space. Thoughts and awarenesses flash across the man's dimmed consciousness — then they disappear. The rolling and twisting edge and slide the man's body across the floor. Light from the window floods his face. He feels heat upon his forehead and sees pink-orange through the front of his skull. He is pleased. He realizes it is the sun. He growls at it and continues the flexing and stretching. He raises up his arms to the sun's heat and feels the warmth on his skin — it seems good and he makes noises at it. He plays in the sun, with eyes still closed, fulfilling the muscle's demands but the sun has awakened consciousness in him. He has shed his human consciousness temporarily but the sun brings back the awareness that he is a being. He feels himself as A MAMMAL! He does not think of himself as MAN but as his weight and size and shape in muscles and organs of sense and consciousness. There is a ball of silence within himself that does not 'judge'; he has touched on it and let himself be what he is when shorn of societal things! He raises up his hands to the sun and with closed eyes sees the blaze of sun colors inside his head. The question of what he is doing pours across his intellect and brings consciousness with it for an instant. He asks himself what he is — he does not know. He is an animal. He is something like . . . Like what? Like a tiger? Like a lion? Yes, he is something like them but he is different. Yes! He knows he is a Man. But he's free of things he must think as a man. The thought — the question — disappears. He has a picture — he sees he is doing what men have done for many thousands of years — falling and praising the sun on their bodies. It is not worship as in a church — it is acknowledgement of the sun. He recognizes it as a power. His intellect returns briefly again. He thinks : ' How normal to admire the sun — the greatest fragment of the universe closest in space. It is the chamber of power from which energy devolves — the plants and creatures welcome its light and live upon the chemical evolutions of light becoming energy . . .' Then he becomes the mammal again and thought disappears. The sun still dazzles his brows. He continues the spontaneous and unsymmetrical exercising but the mammal has become intrigued by light power. In the midst of the stretching he reaches up and tries to part his forehead and the frontal skull. He pulls at it with both hands as if parting a curtain. He holds his forehead up into the direct light of the sun. He presses and tugs back with thumbs and forefingers to spread the screen that keeps his brain from light. He massages the center of the forehead welcoming light. He sees himself doing it. Then awareness slips back and returns again. The exercising continues and he works more on his forehead.

Something flashes into his mind that he has not thought before. It is not the sun that men praise but the thing it represents — REASON! A sentence crosses his mind like a silver ribbon: YES, LET THERE BE LIGHT FOR THE SAKE OF LIGHT! It is not spreading the skull to let in majesty that matters. The majesty, the *reason*, is already there within, changing and being created. Reason is the liberty of human flesh moving in the universe and it is guided by the melodies of truth and honesty. The intellect has nothing to do with reason except that it furnishes the notes by means of which the melody of reason is played in life. Thinking beings orchestrate their lives as a composer does a sonata so that beauty will lend more liberty to the liberty already taken. Reason is a kind of beauty.

The glorious man walking proudly and straightly with shining brows and clean movements — the reasoning man — is not the great thing we picture because of the way he strides or the gestures he makes. Those are outer signs of something physical that is a part of him! If he speaks of 'abstract reason' with beauty and eloquence it is because he already knows reason and may speak in a metaphor or abstraction. He realizes the outer universe is a reflector of his reason!

The wrist may be a sign of reason. There is a certain squareness to my wrist that I study. When I see the wrist become thin and gain a particular angularity I know that I have begun to lose my power of reason. Reason sometimes is nothing more than honesty — the honesty of admissions. The constant making of admissions is one of the forms of honesty. I have noted that when my wrist begins to lose its solidity I become less honest. I have let myself lose some of my youth. Youth is the connection with the universe. The universe is my mother when I am young and may still return to her. Then I am still reasonable.

To a child his mother is Reason — she is what is true and solid. He moves into the world and begins to establish connections. When he is puzzled or frightened he returns to the warmth and breast. Gradually he goes more into the universe and less and less to his mother. The universe gradually becomes his mother — but the universe is what is real to his senses. There is a certain state of his flesh by means of which he relates to reality — and it has nothing to do with his age.

In some men it might be the thinness of their wrists that they use to judge reasonableness. What the physical signs are do not matter as much as their acknowledgement.

Chance and luck are a part of all endeavor. A creature hurt repeatedly by circumstance and chance has less possibility of returning to the universe for his renewal and warmth — he may be cut down in the midst of a farflung action. Such an unlucky man must look to others who have still kept their reason where he has lost, or been cut off from his. But reason comes from within and not from without. It has become a part of the body.

It is the opposition of action to action that is reason. The Greeks said ARISTON METRON — 'moderation is best'. How did they manifest their belief in *ariston metron*? It meant, if we judge by actions, that they went from one extreme to the other — from drunkenness and narcotic exuberance and stupor to sheer meditation, and they found *themselves* in the balance of the possibilities! The middle course is *not* moderation! But the totality of actions that are made in many directions creates moderation, and also beauty, and REASON. Reason is not a narrow course but is ebullience and depression and the states of feeling, and the gestures and the actions that lie between. The man who makes many actions carries them with him in his body and builds his own reason within himself. He takes risks.

No possibility is false — not as long as the admissions come in truthfully through the senses regarding what is there — and why the man sensing it is breathing. In the light of reason everything is to be tested. Man has created the chance of time and space in the image of his eyes, ears and nose. He must be able to slip free of even the images of his creation or they will bind him . . . All states are desirable and there is a physical reason that is his guide through them. Reason is freedom.

CHANCE ! Science says that reality is a series of statistically variable events — and that we react to them with good sense allowing for their predictable totality. Most living beings would never dream the possibility that circumstances might be otherwise than the flow of change.

Sometimes we see possibilities rushing towards us. We watch with open eyes as events come nearer. We sidestep or bring other possibilities into concurrence with the arrival of oncoming events. At the highest pitch of reason WE CREATE EVENT through synthesis of events that we determine and bring into being.

The creative act of reason is a thing done because the human being is overflowing and acts in the manner of a plant, or a star, or animal and procreates itself. The argument that these created events are made because of cause and effect sequences leading to them is wrong. Events that lie in the past need not have to do with the end result of a new creative act or thought put into motion.

The absurdity of Astrology that views stars and planets as inanimate objects controlling our destiny does not negate the possibility that someday we will discover the signs of a super-astrology (*an astrology without rules except for the sense of beauty*) by means of which we will be able in some way to actually feel a relationship of stars and nebulae with our bodies.

Reason is the revolt of the senses against regulations that dull them. The man on the floor allowing his muscles to exercise in answer to an involuntary demand is reasoning. We move among cliffs and icebergs of chance events coming at us. But at the same time we set forth events to meet the forthcoming ones and pick and choose in the ground we inhabit in the present. Sidestepping oncoming events can be just as purposeful an act of reason as any other.

If there is a still higher reason it must be the result of a higher view. Any high view of reality must be a result of the most truthful sights. It could not be the end result of a system attempting to relate life and occurrences to a major pattern formulated from contemporary hopes and ideals.

The man in the sunlight is allowing his muscles to exist more truthfully for what they are. Suddenly in the light of the sun the concept of another reason flashes upon him.

There must be ideals to give strength to courage. But to systematize ideals merely because they are helpful or seem to have a kind of poetics is a trap. There is always a greater beauty possible beyond the boundary of a closed system of thought and feeling. We should leap for it. Poetics does not create beauty but poetry does! Poetry is not a system but is real events spoken of, or happening, in sounds. Poetry is an act of reason at its highest most farflung pitch — and is a demonstration of freedom.

It is the desk, the table, stool, and tree, and glass of water, and our emotions moving upon them that are the actualities of reason. The man exercising on the floor has the most immediate contact of muscle and skin cell to floor and sunlight and commits the basic act of reason. He has momentarily disavowed all modes of thought and forms of seeing. Reason is touch of reality among an infinitude of fantasy possibilities. Choosing the real creates the real when it is done with the senses of the body.

Liberty with the universe springs from the real physical body but it cannot be done well with a bad instrument. *To understand and enlarge their possibilities of reason men enact the most seemingly grotesque and incomprehensible actions.* THESE ACTIONS HAVE BROUGHT THEM INTO CLOSER CONTACT WITH PHYSICAL BEAUTY though it may or may not fit the preconceptions held as popular ideas of their times.

The man on the floor might be the beginning of a Christ or a Buddha or a Faraday. He has allowed himself to be the unthinking creature and the beginning of reason comes to him. He lets himself exist in the world of darkness before there is reason and reason flashes into it. The demarcation between a reasonable and an unreasonable act rests on whether the thing that causes the action exists in actuality or not — it is a matter of creating among possibilities.

II

What comes straight in through the senses and combines with imagination without distortion is the concrete reality on which reason is based. The drunkenness of a man at a banquet who will, the next day, spend time in thought and exercise is not the same drunkenness as the man who is drunk one day and the next and the next . . . Though even that in view of the chances of life, is conceivably a reasonable act. There must be joy and pleasure in reason! If there is not pleasure in life then there will be less energy and less energy in life is less life. When ' reason ' is a strait jacket it is an evasion of what is truly reason.

Logic is a system to increase the strength of the most fearful members of society and it gives them an overweening lever on the thoughts of the less fearful. Reason is a revolt from the projections of the unreal that are cast upon the world. Logic is an unreal projection and has no relationship to reason. We live in a sequence of happenings that is sheer beauty — except when we distort it.

Obsessive concern for the correctness of details is not Reason. The recognition of the reality of event is Reason. The man rolling on the floor does not count the floor boards with the skin of his arms nor estimate the number of light beams falling upon him. He feels the heat of light and the hardness of floor and the multitudinous events of reality in which he moves. In society he sees the events in his milieu and also the events he sidesteps and sets into motion. These are physical things in time and space and he recognizes their relationships. REASON IS NOT THE DEMARCATION OF A NARROW TRAIL OF LOGIC. NO MAN IS HUMANLY ABOVE THE VARIATIONS OF CHANCE OR WOULD WILLFULLY BLIND HIMSELF TO THE SPONTANEOUS HAPPEN- INGS AND CHANGES OF BEAUTIES SURROUNDING HIM AND OCCURRING WITHIN HIMSELF. REASON IS THE ASSUMPTION OF THE POSSIBILITIES IN THE DRAMA. Besides moving among events the man of reason must move along with him as many sights as he can accept and make a part of his reasoning. The man of reason, though his eyes be looking either inward or outward, is a cyclone of what he has known, felt, and seen. He does not deny those things to fit laws of Platonism and logic.

Reason does not need to give offense or point to itself. The man of reason is not in error when he is accused of misjudge- ment — he is keeping alive a natural process in his body! Reason takes into account the naturalness of others and honors them.

The man on the floor does not give offense except to those

who fear what he experiences. Fearful ones can always find a criminal name to apply to any act. The man who looks to his own body for signs of reason or lack of reason must generally not speak of it. Those who have gone insane or had spiritual cataclysms and illuminations of tenderness or fear are often pursuing Reason — Society does not like to hear of it for the reasoners have gone too far. Yet when those men deliberately pursue REASON Society must accept the discoveries into the balance of possible societal acts — the meaning of the word Reason becomes broadened by the extremes that men enact. At this point REASON becomes physical acts. All men are men of reason and they are unaware of it because of a silence that has become a tenet. All that happens to a man is reality.

The man of reason is the one who denies the smallest possible number of things that have occurred in his existence . . . Yet he has the power, when he needs it, to cancel out what memories and personal past happenings would prevent him from achieving a goal. He is capable of analyzing sequences of events to a fine state and through internal revolutions — even to the mutation of the nerves of his body through chemicals and intense emotion — adapt himself for as long as necessary to a planned and changing pattern of creations that finally arrive at the fulfillment of an ideal. The most brilliant reasoners have been able to allow for a high degree of chance. Reason is a physical process felt kinesthetically by the body.

How can Reason be separated from the meat — except temporarily by an act of will? All that is experienced, without being twisted into the shape of preconceptions, is REASON. The energetic acceptance of life is one of the shapes of understanding and is Reason. The ability to simultaneously choose and guide one's self amongst acts is an amplification of Reason. Living constantly in a preconceived and straitened pattern of life is not Reason . . . it has no balance. *Ariston metron* must mean the ability to hold everything at once and acknowledge it all as true and still keep it viable and flexible. Men who do this are called *lucky*. Surely it is LUCK! There may be a genetic basis to luck with causations so minute and biochemical that we shall not unravel them for a hundred years. *Chance* and *Luck* are joys and virtues in a lovely game and drama.

If the man on the floor should vomit from his release of tension and to clear and purify his senses (as an extension of his motions) it is an act of reason. Reason is not a part of temporal manners.

Reason is the ability to shed the knowledge of being a man — like the man on the floor does — and to exist in the universe as a living and free part. There must be the knowledge of what the body is — the image it makes in matter and energy — and the entities that comprise it. Reason is a shedding of the mundane view and its restrictions.

Reasoning deals with stark reality in any shape that it may exist, but the 'human aspect' is sheerest veneer in the huger meaning of what a human being is. There is a greater mass of loves and structurings and emotions and hopes. Reason does not bow to the veneer but is as impetuous and calculated as love is. The thin layer constantly acknowledged on the face of human activities is devoid of human and animal meaning *except for what lies beneath it and the reality of events that it encompasses* . . . Reason works among events and gesture and reality. The man on the floor is partly in that place. The man of reason occupies both the real physical world and the world of manners simultaneously and without contradiction. They are complementary for him and no distinction is necessary. He devotes himself to honesty and the necessity of constant admissions. It is the confrontation of the world in all of its shapes that is reason.

The man on the floor stretching leg over leg snarls the mammal sounds in the sunlight — he twists his body to exert the sleeping muscles and he groans. It is impossible to believe that

there are 'levels of existence' — a kind of modern psychological folklore — but there ARE secret hopes and desires and
always have been. The man twisting the muscles of spine
and crushing his shoulders against the boards of the floor is
acknowledging them.

*The context of an act of reason and the goals of reason
may make Reason illogical!* Logic demands that the passage
of cause & effect fit a preconception. The man making rhythms
with his body in space relates himself to all constructions of
physical matter in the universe . . . His physical act is a por-
trayal of his belief that matter is spirit and that meat is the
container. Boughs of the evergreens moving in the wind relate
to him in Reason. The laughter of the onlooker is a relationship of reason. The man needs no logic, but stretching his leg
and twisting the muscles of his arm in pleasure creates reason.
The pearl gleaming on flesh in the light is an act of reason!

' The Essays are explorations and trials arising out of eight or nine years of continual revolt and transformation. . . . Michael McClure's poetry and prose is one of the more remarkable achievements in recent American literature. . . .'

  — *The London Times Literary Supplement*